Thomas Campbell

*Seceder and Christian
Union Advocate*

... BY ...

WILLIAM HERBERT HANNA

PUBLISHERS
Eugene, Oregon

Wipf and Stock Publishers
199 W 8th Ave, Suite 3
Eugene, OR 97401

Thomas Campbell
Seceder and Christian Union Advocate
By Hanna, William Herbert
ISBN 13: 978-1-55635-414-14
ISBN 10: 1-55635-414-2
Publication date 4/7/2007
Previously published by Standard Publishing, 1935

DEDICATION

To her, beloved fellow worker in the gospel of Christ for three and a half decades in both Occident and Orient—my wife

FOREWORD

IT is a distinct pleasure to write a word concerning the significance and value of the pages which follow. In the judgment of the writer, no more valuable contribution to the early history of the Disciples of Christ has been made since the publication of Robert Richardson's *Memoirs of Alexander Campbell*. The source material contained in this book is of the highest value and serves as a corrective in certain particulars of even such authoritative biographers as Richardson and Alexander Campbell. The fact is that the latter depended upon his memory too exclusively and made frequent errors on this account. The main facts, of course, remain unchanged, but some very important details are set forth in a new light, so that the total picture is made more brilliant and luminous. Thomas Campbell becomes a much more lifelike figure than he had been before, and the action of the Associate Synod of North America likewise becomes much more explicable when its official minutes are read and studied. Mr. Campbell was obviously a little petulant and the Synod was likewise doing its best to reach a decision satisfactory to all parties. The whole situation, as Mr. Hanna discloses it to us, is decidedly human, dramatic and convincing. We recognize the personal motives back of the unwarranted persecution of the Chartiers Presbytery, and it is perfectly clear that the officials of the Synod of North America saw through the situation also. At the same time they were quite justly suspicious of Thomas Campbell's orthodoxy, and their analysis of his theological position was, in the main, clear and sound. Campbell himself at this time appears to have been feeling his way, and, no doubt, failed to appreciate the full implications of his teaching. It required the bitter experience of censure and suspension on the part of the two ecclesiastical bodies to ripen his thinking into the full fruition of the "Declaration and Address." "God moves in a mysterious way his wonders to perform." If the Seceders had been a little more tolerant, the "Declaration and Address" would probably never have been written.

Up until the appearance of this volume no satisfactory biography of Thomas Campbell has been available. The memoirs written by his son, as the author of the present book indicates, never met with public approval, and today only a few scattered copies are in existence. The reasons assigned for the inadequacy of the work by its author are no doubt partially correct, but they do not seem to cover the entire ground. The truth appears to be that Alexander Campbell, when he undertook the job, was aging rapidly, his memory was failing, and there was something about the whole situation which made the task entirely hopeless for him. In the prime of his life he would have produced a great interpretation of his father's career, but when he set his hand to the undertaking he was no longer capable of measuring up to the responsibility which was laid upon him. Nevertheless, just because he was Alexander Campbell, and because he had written at least a purported biography of his father, later writers felt estopped from touching the subject. For this reason, perhaps more than any other, Thomas Campbell has remained without an adequate biography until Mr. Hanna, inspired by the discovery of his new source material, essayed the task. He has thus placed all of us under a debt of gratitude for filling in a gap which threatened to become permanent.

One word more may be added concerning the immense value of preserving what may sometimes appear to be unimportant and uninteresting records. Perhaps to most people the minutes of the Chartiers Presbytery, written over a hundred years ago, would seem to be singularly inconsequential. The Campbell case was only one out of a number of similar instances of routine procedure which even to contemporaries were probably tiresome enough. We read them today with intense interest because of what history has done for some of the characters who are involved. The moral would appear to be that no transactions of any organization should be regarded as unworthy of preservation. It is highly desirable that future generations should understand the facts of past history in order the more surely to expand their own outlook. Accurate and detailed official records help to promote such an understanding more than anything else. We must be sincerely grateful today to the men who wrote and preserved the records upon which the present volume is so largely based, and to the author of this book for making them available for the general public.

It scarcely seems necessary to call attention to the fact that Mr. Hanna has once and for all laid the ghost of the imaginative schism between Thomas and Alexander Campbell which has been advocated at times by uninformed radicals. On only one or two rather unimportant matters was there any real difference of opinion between father and son throughout the long period of their harmonious and co-operative fellowship. The fact is that Alexander carried out the plan and program of his father to the very best of his extraordinary ability. Thomas Campbell, on the other hand, was delighted at the forensic leadership of his son and was content to remain in the background so long as the principles which he advocated were being promulgated in such admirable fashion. History records few instances of more thoroughgoing and consistent harmony between two great leaders in the work of the church. The famous relationship which existed between Luther and Melanchthon was far less ideal. Not the least service of the present volume is the fact that it helps to immortalize the sacred and beautiful unity of spirit which existed between Father Campbell and his illustrious son and successor.

FREDERICK D. KERSHNER.

BUTLER UNIVERSITY,
Indianapolis, Ind.
2nd of September, 1935.

CONTENTS

Introduction 15

I

FROM IRELAND TO AMERICA

Notes on family history—Early religious life—Education in Glasgow University and Anti-Burgher Seminary—Marriage —First charge and lines of work pursued—Sickness and decision to go to America—Seated in Synod—Assignment of field of service.. 23

II

HERETICAL TEACHINGS DISCOVERED

Beginnings of connection with Chartiers Presbytery—The schedule of services among the churches—Rumblings as to heretical teachings—Committee appointed to investigate— Libel for heresy in seven respects returned—Thomas Campbell handed the Libel and method of trial determined upon— Barred from ministerial service.. 31

III

PRESBYTERY UPHOLDS HERESY LIBEL

The trial before Presbytery—Mr. Campbell's answers— Testimony of various witnesses—Adjudged guilty and suspended from ministerial work sine die—Mr. Campbell protests procedure of Presbytery and appeals to Synod.................. 45

IV

SYNOD REVERSES PRESBYTERY IN PART

Protest and appeal of Thomas Campbell to Synod—Petitions from friends to Synod—Judgment of Presbytery reversed—Suspension sustained—Synod hears accused on various items of the Libel—Synod appoints committee to bring in a report—Report received—Mr. Campbell objects to report and is permitted to state his faith as to items involved—Virtually clears himself of leading charges—Report amended, but accused is rebuked and admonished—Appointment for two months in Presbytery of Philadelphia.. 68

V

FAREWELL TO SECEDERISM

Dissatisfaction of Chartiers Presbytery with action of Synod—Sharp disagreement of Mr. Campbell and Presbytery as to minutes of Synod—He declines authority of both Presbytery and Synod—Attends Synod that met in May of 1809—Repays money advanced him in 1807—Finally deposed and suspended from sealing ordinances—Examination of sketch of Thomas Campbell in "United Presbyterian Manual".................. 86

VI

ONE SHIP ARRIVES

The family in Ireland sets out for New World—Shipwrecked—Takes up temporary residence in Glasgow—Alexander Campbell in the university—A second embarkment to meet the father—Voyage and arrival.. 101

VII

EXAMINATION OF AN "ADDRESS"

Question of date of separation from Secederism—A letter and protest to Synod—Internal evidence shows the letter to be other than his son thought it to be.. 106

VIII

A NEW TITLE AND A GREAT MOTTO

A new title for Thomas Campbell—Previous interest in union of churches—New and enlarged conception of Christian

CONTENTS 11

union—The overlooked petitions of friends—Preaching widely as God's free man—Startling announcement of the rule "Where the Scriptures speak, we speak; where the Scriptures are silent, we are silent".. 112

IX

CHRISTIAN ASSOCIATION—ITS DECLARATION

The formation of the Christian Association of Washington —Writing and publication of "Declaration and Address"— The contents—Abbreviated principles of Address—The Appendix—Some men of olden time who wrote as did Thomas Campbell 118

X

FATHER AND SON JOIN FORCES

Meeting of father and son after long separation—Latter's first hearing of Declaration and Address—Father begins to train preachers—Overtures to Synod of Pittsburgh and rejection—Relation to parties—Removal from town of Washington —Christian Association becomes a church—Thomas Campbell's first immersions—Famous immersion of seven in a seven-hour service—Brush Run Church becomes one of immersed believers 125

XI

FELLOWSHIP WITH BAPTIST ASSOCIATION

Alexander Campbell ordained—Legal record made of same —Joint services of father and son—Acquaintance with Baptist Churches—Brush Run Church enters Redstone Baptist Association guardedly—Extent of the Campbells' faith in Baptist principles—Thomas Campbell's Ohio academy—Academy in Pittsburgh—Campbell's new church in Pittsburgh denied place in Redstone Association—Remarkable thesis on the Trinity...... 133

XII

FROM KENTUCKY BACK TO PENNSYLVANIA

Thomas Campbell becomes educator and preacher in Kentucky—Experience with slaves and slave laws—Returns hastily to Pennsylvania and begins to assist in Buffaloe Academy—A gratified hearer of his son's debate with Walker—The Mahoning Association—Scheme of Redstone Association to oust the Campbells is foiled—The church of Christ in Wellsburg..... 141

XIII

APOSTOLIC DOCTRINE BY PEN AND VOICE

The Christian Baptist launched—Brush Run Church expelled from Redstone Association—Becomes a part of new Association of Washington—Brush Run merges with Bethany—Thomas Campbell and son (A. W.) itinerate in Ohio and western Pennsylvania—Walter Scott becomes evangelist of Mahoning Association—Thomas Campbell sent to investigate doctrine and methods of Scott—Heartily endorses—Some men touched by the elder Campbell.. 147

XIV

SOCIALISM—MILLENNIALISM—MORMONISM

Acquaintance of father Campbell with Robert Owen—Some service in Cincinnati—Note about Elkhorn Association in Kentucky—The Campbells defend Cyrus McNeely—"Reformers" augmented by Baptists in many places—Rise of name "Campbellite"—Extract from letter written in Kentucky by Mr. Campbell to his wife—The Millennium—*The Millennial Harbinger* projected—Rise of Mormonism—Thomas Campbell visits its Ohio center and challenges Sidney Rigdon to debate.. 155

XV

NAME—NEW NEW TESTAMENT—BEREAVEMENT

A peacemaker in the churches—Instance of reproving error in preaching—Independence of mind of both Campbells—

CONTENTS 13

The older Campbell agrees with Stone as to name "Christian" —Tour of Baptist churches in Virginia—A. Campbell's new version of the New Testament—Father Campbell's part in the new work—His relation to Christians growing out of Barton W. Stone's work—His strictures on Stone's teaching on the Atonement—Horseback tour of Virginia and North Carolina—Baptist resolution in latter state against Thomas Campbell, "teacher of Campbellism"—Edits *Millennial Harbinger* for seventy-five days—Death of his wife.. 162

XVI

A WATCHFUL EYE ON THE REFORMATION

Letter to "My Dear Son" published in *Harbinger*—Attends to the magazine—Writes on "Divine Order for Evangelizing the World"—A church program and church book for roll of members and finances—Examines at length a Christian union method launched in New York—Favors his own............ 174

XVII

EDUCATION, HIGHER AND FAMILY—SLAVERY

Bethany College comes into being—Thomas Campbell on Board of Trustees—Article on "Family Education—The Nursery"—An index to the study and teaching of the Bible—The long and vexing question of slavery—Correcting false impressions as to the Campbells' attitude... 182

XVIII

ZEALOUS EVEN UNTO DEATH

Evangelizes in Ohio in 1843—A letter touching relations with the Baptists—Heartfelt religion under "The Actual Enjoyment of Religion"—Letter to converted infidel about to start evangelizing in New England—Thomas Henley's appreciative word—The last itinerary of Thomas Campbell—Final public address in the Bethany Church—Death and burial........ 190

XIX

SOME TRIBUTES FROM ADMIRERS

Obituary notices—Appreciations by Dr. Richardson and son Alexander—Account of James Challen's visit to Thomas Campbell—Letter and tribute of Walter Scott—The reformer reforms from snuff—Scott and A. McLean agree as to Thomas Campbell's insensibility to time—Long prayer while a divinity student gets him a caning.. 198

XX

CHARACTER—CONSISTENCY—THE FELLOWSHIP

Summary of the son's appreciation of his father—Latter always interested in young men—Clarity of mental and spiritual vision—Discouragement always found a supply of patience—The place of immersion in the union plan—Dared to become consistent—Particular esteem for Baptists and probable reason—Two sets of fellowship that hark back to Declaration and Address—A party to end parties in Christianity.... 207

XXI

THE PLEA AND PLAN: AMEND OR ADOPT?

New divisions and denominations since Campbell's call to union—Position of creeds in churches today—Recent plans for co-operation and union—Some denominational alliances and unions—Projected unions—Debt to Thomas Campbell—His plan valid for this time—Pertinent quotations from original document—The place of authority—The noble man and his heaven-born desire... 215

INTRODUCTION

THOMAS CAMPBELL died on Jan. 4, 1854. His friends and relatives felt that there ought to be a biography of him whose life had been long, worthy and inseparably connected with the religious movement that was making so great a challenge to American and even European life. It was believed that there could be no better person to make Thomas Campbell live through a biography than his son, Alexander. This son had more than the usual pride of a son in his father, and sensed the duty to memorialize him in a book. Notwithstanding what seemed to be an urgent call for an immediate performance of this act, it was not until the year of 1861 that Alexander Campbell published under copyright a book entitled *Memoirs of Elder Thomas Campbell*. From the preface we take this closing paragraph: "This memoir has long been called for. My apology is and has been, the multiplicity and the variety of public calls upon my time at home and abroad, in connection with the Bible Union, Bethany College, and my long tours in response to many calls and importunities. I have long been waiting for a more convenient season, but it still seemed to be in the future. And even now, at last, I have to regret that it had to be dispatched in too much haste to satisfy my own intention and desire. But, under all the circumstances that surround me and all the duties incumbent upon me, I have done the best I could."

The reader of the resultant *Memoirs* is sure to be just as much dissatisfied with it as its writer declares he was. So intimate had been the association of the father, Thomas Campbell, and the son, Alexander, for fifty-odd years, that the latter was the only one qualified to preserve the life of his father and make him an intimate friend of succeeding generations of men. Even though the elder Campbell had tens of thousands of admirers in all parts of the world, the *Memoirs* made but little appeal to them. It lacked so much of being a "life"; never had a wide circulation; and there is no record that a second edition was ever called for. The biographer delegated to his brother the task of writing of "a certain period of Father Campbell's life and labors" on the ground that he was more conversant with the same, with the result that Dr. Archibald Campbell is as much the writer of the above-mentioned *Memoirs* as Alexander. Yet we are able to enjoy the little that was presented by both, together with a few letters, a glimpse into Thomas Campbell's diary for 1800, magazine articles, and letters of appreciation that came upon the death of him whom they had come to esteem for his works' sake in the restoration of primitive Christianity.

To the *Memoirs of Alexander Campbell,* by Dr. Robert Richardson, the world owes far more of its knowledge of Thomas Campbell than to any other work. This two-volume work is so exhaustive

INTRODUCTION 17

and charming that it has become monumental. Its length has made it a mark for abbreviators. Other lives of Alexander Campbell have been written since, but they all lean hard on Richardson and have little original material. No person has thought it worth while to attempt another life of Thomas Campbell, though Dr. Richardson adds very much to the data found in *Memoirs of Thomas Campbell*. The lamented Archibald McLean prepared two addresses on the Campbells, father and son, and had them published in a booklet under the name *Thomas and Alexander Campbell*. The edition was small, and can not be looked upon as other than a tribute and interpretation. It is possible that the paucity of material has warned writers away from Thomas Campbell as a subject. However, some genius may arise one day to give to the world a more extended and satisfactory account of the life and labors of the truly great Christian and religious leader that he was.

The present work is not to be esteemed as the offering of a master. The writer counts himself but a student of his subject. In connection with finishing work leading to a degree in Western Theological Seminary, some themes were called for. Among subjects chosen were "Thomas Campbell: Seceder" and "Thomas Campbell: Advocate of Christian Union." These were approved by the professor of church history, and work was begun upon them. It occurred to the aspirant that neither Doctor Richardson nor any other writer, so far as known, had made use of documentary material from

Presbyterian sources. It may be that it was not available, or that they had not thought of its existence. At any rate, the two documents that relate to the American life of Thomas Campbell as a Seceder minister and are necessary source material are "Minutes of Chartiers Presbytery" and "Minutes of Associate Synod of North America," both of which embrace the years from 1807 to 1810. These books, in the original handwriting of the secretaries of the respective bodies are now in the archives of the Library of the Pittsburgh-Xenia Theological Seminary, located at Pittsburgh, Pa. They are books, blank books once, and bear evidence of having been used and examined in the course of years. Possibly it was by those who were interested in Secederism and United Presbyterianism. Or it may be that persons interested in the Campbellian movement had used the works, but little direct use of the same has been indicated in any publications that have come to the attention of the writer.

It is possible that an apology ought to be made for making such liberal use of the actual words and form of the two sets of minutes. The writer's thought has been to multiply copies of the material that concerns Thomas Campbell, for those original documents will likely never be published. The secretaries of Chartiers Presbytery and of the Associate Synod were not composing literature, but they were writing happenings, reporting acts and speeches of deliberative bodies, and theirs was a hard task. None were shorthand reporters; they had no typewriters, no fountain pens, no steel pens, no blotting paper. It is not to be wondered at that a secretary of an organization in the early part of 1800 would write as little as he could and abbreviate where he thought it wise, and endeavor to condense as much as possible. On two occasions, at least, Thomas Campbell was led to question the accuracy of the minutes as well as their completeness. Several times we discover Mr. Campbell moved to "crave extracts" from the minutes. As one reads the minutes of those happenings in ecclesiastical circles of more than a century and a quarter ago, he discovers how earnestly the things of religion were dealt with.

Aside from places where Thomas Campbell's matters appear, we find things that are of interest to us. The Chartiers Presbytery had its problems with ministers who walked disorderly, presbyters who opposed ministers, who slandered, kept back wages and so on. In that early period both Presbytery and Synod were making resolutions concerning slavery. Such records help to give us the background of the period, and Thomas Campbell was in the midst of it all. An effort has been made, however, to copy in exact detail what concerned him most intimately during the period when he professed allegiance to Chartiers Presbytery and the Associate Synod.

It has been with some temerity that corrections have been offered on the report of the heresy trial of Mr. Campbell as it has been written up by Dr. Richardson. By no means would the latter be charged with inaccuracy. He seems to have been dependent on the recollections of both Thomas Campbell and Alexander. Both of them had either forgotten some of the details or possibly had not thought they were of sufficient importance to mention. The records bear witness to the fact that the heresy trial was based on something more than the charge of a single minister that the accused was irregular in ecclesiastical procedure and errant in some teaching. The libel is almost ponderous in its seven items and the sevenfold recurrence of the refrain, "but you, the Rev'd Thomas Campbell." But Mr. Campbell does not suffer from the very intimate view we get of him before presbyters and fellow ministers as he sought to justify himself. On several occasions we are told that Mr. Campbell withdrew from both Presbytery and Synod, refusing to sit longer in the session. It was not petulance at being opposed that so moved him, but a sense that right and justice were being outraged. But the reader must be left to assess the conduct and stand of "Thomas Campbell: Seceder," as he feels the record demands.

A new era in the life of Mr. Campbell set in when he, having separated from Secederism, took his position for Christian union. As we enter into that era we discover that we are very largely indebted to *Memoirs* by Dr. Richardson for a record of the elder Campbell's activities. Too often, it seems to the writer, sufficient place is not given to Alexander Campbell's father. We dare not blame the great biographer, for he was writing chiefly about the son. Would that he had essayed another "Memoirs" and given Thomas Campbell the prominence he deserved in the "Current Reformation." It is the desire of the author (utilizing materials in *Memoirs of Thomas Campbell,* the *Christian Baptist* and the *Millennial Harbinger* and one or two other works) to lift "father" Campbell into greater prominence, out of some of the shade into which the greatness of his son has thrust him. Nothing is to be taken from the halo of genuine greatness that has been placed upon the brow of Alexander Campbell. It may be that church historians have failed to construct the full halo which Thomas Campbell deserves. There is far more owing him than the great honor of having produced the "Declaration and Address." A humble effort has been made to set forth in somewhat clear, but not exhaustive, fashion the life period from 1810 until 1854, during which Thomas Campbell deserves to be known as "Advocate of Christian Union." If this work shall spur some one to write an adequate biography, the writer will rejoice. If readers will be moved to thank God anew for such a character as Thomas Campbell and will be tracing yet his service and influence in the great task of bringing together all those who call upon the name of the Lord Jesus Christ, they will give the writer his reward. It has been a joy to go with Thomas Campbell through his ninety-one years. THE AUTHOR.

Chapter I

FROM IRELAND TO AMERICA

THE father of Thomas Campbell, Archibald Campbell, traced his lineage back to the race of Diarmid, the Campbells of Argyleshire, Scotland, but he was born in County Down, near Dyerlake, Ireland. The life of a soldier appealed to him, and it fell to his lot to serve under General Wolfe at the battle of Quebec. Alexander Campbell (*Memoirs of Elder Thomas Campbell,* p. 7) refers to the tradition that General Wolfe died in the arms of Archibald Campbell, his grandfather. After that famous battle, he returned home to Ireland and established himself near Newry, County Down. He married and four sons were born. A great religious change took place also in the life of the old soldier. He had been a Roman Catholic, but was converted from that faith, by what process we know not. He became a strict member of the Church of England, and died in his eighty-eighth year, a firm adherent of the same. None of his four sons chose to "serve God according to the Act of Parliament" as their father was accustomed to put it. The three of them, who lived to maturity, cast in their lot with the Secession Church. These three were alike also in following the teaching profession in their early years.

Thomas Campbell was the oldest son of Archibald Campbell, and came to fame in the ministry of the gospel. Rather early in life "he became the subject of deep religious impressions, and acquired a most sincere and earnest love for the Scriptures." From Richardson's *Memoirs of Alexander Campbell* (pp. 21, 22) we learn that young Thomas preferred, above the formality of ritualism, the society of the rigid and devotional Covenanters and began to worship with them. His own personal salvation gave him deep concern as he grew older. Friends endeavored to guide him with their counsel; he made use of prayer with earnestness and diligence, and he sought for such assurance of forgiveness and acceptance as he felt ought to come as the accompaniments of true faith and effectual calling. One day as he was walking in the fields alone and meditating, "he felt a divine peace suddenly diffuse itself throughout his soul, and the love of God seemed to be shed abroad in his heart as he had never before realized it." Richardson continues (*ibid.*, p. 23), "His doubts, anxieties and fears were at once dissipated, as if by enchantment. . . . From this moment he recognized himself as consecrated to God, and thought only how he might best appropriate his time and his abilities to His service." Together with this which may be called the conversion of Thomas Campbell there came simultaneously the feeling that he had been called to be a minister. In dutiful fashion, the son informed his father of the desire of his heart to become a minister of the gospel in the Seceder Branch of the Church of Scotland. Details are lacking of the interview, but it is known that the father was intensely displeased. Through later conversations, the unalterable intention of the son was revealed, and ultimately the father gave a somewhat grudging consent.

Before actually beginning his ministerial studies, Thomas Campbell made two excursions into the field of teaching. First, he went to the south of Ireland in the province of Connaught. From there his father summoned him back home, and he began to teach in a school at Sheepbridge, near Newry. He had been born Feb. 1, 1763, and was beginning to feel that he ought to begin his theological studies at this time, for he was late in his teens. A Mr. John Kinley, who had come to know the young man and esteem his abilities highly, urged him to go to Glasgow, and offered to defray the expenses of his education there. The father was won over to the project, and Thomas proceeded to the University of Glasgow. He took the three years of prescribed study at that time for students of divinity, and also attended medical lectures which were offered then for those who would become ministers, so that they could aid the poorer of their parishioners. His pursuit of the regular theological studies followed in the Anti-Burgher School. This was located at Whitburn, and its teacher was Rev. Archibald Bruce, a man well qualified, of piety and some renown, and esteemed by the students. There were five annual sessions of eight weeks each, and all subjects were taught by a single professor. The enrollment at that period was between twenty and thirty students. The period of study ended, Thomas Campbell submitted to the usual examination and trials for license before the Presbytery of Ireland, and became a probationer with the rights to preach under the supervision of the Synod. In the capacity of probationer, he preached for the churches in the neighborhood of Sheepbridge. He also resumed teaching school. Even before his graduation it would seem that Thomas Campbell married Jane Corneigle, surely in the year of 1787 (dates on this period are uncertain, for family records were lost in a shipwreck). Later he went to Market Hill in County Armagh, and labored as both teacher and probationer. About the year 1798, he accepted a call from a newly established church at Ahorey, some four miles from the city of Armagh. He located himself and the growing family on a farm and began a ministry that was happy and fruitful. He later established an academy and conducted it in his own home at Rich Hill, for farming had not paid.

Thomas Campbell went beyond the usual services that a minister rendered to his people, and gave himself "in preaching, teaching and in visiting his charge, inculcating personal and family religion" so that his son estimates that his father had no equal, nor indeed a superior (*Memoirs of Elder Thomas Campbell*, p. 9). Among other things, he addressed himself to the reunion of the two sects of Burghers. The oath was inconsequential in Ireland, and he felt that the two bodies ought to be one in that country. The people most concerned about it, the Seceders of Ireland, were ready for the step, and sent Thomas Campbell to the Synod to present their case. Notwithstanding his earnestness and force, the Synod at Glasgow decided to leave matters as they had been in Ireland. However, the questions that had been agitated later came to the fore, even in Scotland, and what Thomas Campbell had helped to prepare for and urged in 1806, was consummated on Sept. 5, 1820 —the union of the two Synods, Burgher and Anti-Burgher. This took place in the very church house and city of Edinburgh, where the division had occurred seventy-five years before (*Memoirs of Alexander Campbell,* pp. 57, 58).

As he pursued his ministerial work, Thomas Campbell developed a stomach trouble that gave him much discomfort and anxiety. He sought the aid of physicians, but they were unable to afford him relief. As a last resort it was suggested that he try a sea voyage and a complete rest from pastoral cares. Mr. Campbell accepted the prescription, and turned his eyes longingly to America in the New World. The fact that his eldest son, Alexander, had already declared his intention of making America his home, when he should attain his majority, which would indicate that there had been family discussions as to the United States and its political and religious ideals. Some of the friends and parishioners of the father had left the region and gone to try their fortunes in the New World. They had made Washington County, Pennsylvania, their home. Quite naturally, therefore, the ailing minister chose as his journey's end the section of country where friends were located. Moreover, he seems to have set forth with the determination to settle permanently in America if he found things to his liking. The welfare of the family he was leaving behind for a time, Mr. Campbell committed to God and his eldest son. Armed with a certificate of church membership and of ministerial standing, with his Bible and possibly a few other books, he set sail from Londonderry. After an expeditious voyage of thirty-five days, the vessel brought the Scotch-Irish Seceder minister to the port of Philadelphia.

Providentially, he found the Synod of North America in session there, and on the second day after his arrival, Thomas Campbell presented himself and his credential:

"We, the remainent members of the Presbytery at Market Hall, March 24th, A. D. 1807, do hereby certify that the bearer, Thomas Campbell, has been for about nine years minister of the gospel in the seceding congregation of Ahorey, and co-presbyter with us, during which time he has maintained an irreproachable moral character; and, in the discharge of the duties of his sacred functions has conducted himself as a faithful minister of Christ; and is now released from his pastoral charge over said congregation at his own request, upon good and sufficient reasons for his resignation of said charge, particularly his intention of going to America.

"Given under our hands at our presbyterial meeting, the day and year above written.

"The above, by order of Presbytery, is subscribed by DAVID ARROTT, Moderator."
(*Memoirs of Elder Thomas Campbell*, p. 20.)

Some resolutions of the Synod on the morning of May 14, 1807, are of concern to us:

"1. That a fund be established for defraying the expenses of distant members traveling to Synod.

"2. A fund be established for regularly and promptly paying the passage of ministers from Scotland.

"3. That ministers take into consideration of organizing themselves for the relief of the aged and sick members, and for the widows of members."

There was also a memorial from Chartiers Presbytery which indicated that there was some trouble in the congregation at Buffalo over elders and a minister whose services were declined. In the minutes of the session held "Sat. 16. May," at half-past two in the afternoon, we read, "Mr. Thomas Campbell, minister from Associate Presbytery of Market Hill, Ireland, presented a certificate subscribed by Mr. David Arrott as Mod'r of said Presb'y. He was received into Christian and ministerial communion; and his name being added to the roll, was admitted to a seat in the Synod."

The scheme of appointments was presented to Synod on Monday, May 18. . . ."Mr. Thos. Campbell in the Presb'y of Chartiers and likewise, Mr. John Dickie, till next meeting. This appointment, however, subject to the order following: That the Presbytery of Chartiers, according to the information that they shall receive from the brethren of the Presb'y of the Carolinas, pointing the propriety of the measure, shall send either Mr. Campbell or Mr. Dickie to supply there in the fall."

In the minutes of the session of Synod at 3 p. m. on May 20, 1807, there is found: "After some conversation, respecting the assistance to be allowed Messrs. Campbell and Dickie for equipping them for taking journey in order to fulfill their appointments, it was agreed to allow each of them fifty dollars." ("Minutes of Associate Synod of North America.")

Chapter II

HERETICAL TEACHINGS DISCOVERED

MR. CAMPBELL endeavored to keep his family aware of his goings, but some of the letters that deal with the things of the Synod and of the journey to his new place of labor in Washington County, Pa., failed to reach their destination. However, the family learned of his appointment and the early satisfaction he had in his ministry.

The "Minutes of Chartiers Presbytery" contain no formal notice of the entrance of Messrs. Campbell and Dickie into its boundaries and fellowship. It is naturally concluded that he was present for the first time at the Presbytery session held at the Harmony Meeting-house, June 30 and July 1, 1807. Though Mr. Campbell's name does not occur as listed among those present, he is given assignments as follows: "Mr. Campbell at Buffaloe on the 2d and 3d sab. of July, at Mt. Pleasant on the 4th, at Pittsburgh on 1st sab. of August; at Squire McKees on the 2d; at Cannamaugh on the 3rd and 4th, at Squire Smith's on 5th, at John Templeton's on the 1st sab. of Sept'r, at Upper Piney Creek in John Sloane's on the 2d, at Mercer's on the 3rd and 4th, at John Hammel's on the 1st of Oct'r, at Breakneck on the 2nd and at Buffaloe on the 3rd and 4th" (p. 122).

In *Memoirs of Elder Campbell,* Alexander Campbell offers selections from his father's diary, acquainting us with his habit of keeping such a book. These extracts bear dates in the year of 1800 only. Unfortunately there is no diary, nor are there letters extant that cover the period of life with which we are dealing. How Mr. Campbell went to these appointments, which took him into Beaver, Allegheny and Indiana Counties of Pennsylvania, as well as in his own home county of Washington, we know not. Probably he rode horseback as he surely did some twenty years later; for a writer refers to the old sorrel Thomas Campbell used on trips to Ohio. Stagecoach and canal boat were at times available. Occasionally the preachers in the Chartiers Presbytery failed to meet their engagements, and they were expected to give satisfactory reasons for such failures. Note this extract from the minutes of June 30, 1807: "Mr. Duncan offered objections against his preaching according to the appointment of last meeting; but his objection not being admitted, it was agreed that after the space of half an hour he should go out and preach a sermon, which he accordingly did." One can not but wonder whether Mr. Duncan preached to people or cattle and sheep or to a grove of oak trees.

We will search in vain for any report or intimation that Mr. Campbell failed to meet any of his appointments. But it was the failure of the Rev. Mr. Anderson which brought forth the first *detailed* heresy trial in the United States. Chartiers Presbytery met at Mt. Hope Meeting-house on Oct. 27, 1807, and Thos. Campbell's name (spelled almost without exception in the Minutes with but one l) is listed among the ministers present. "Enquiry having been made concerning the fulfillment of appointments, Mr. Anderson acknowledged that he had not fulfilled the appointment to assist Mr. Campbel in dispensing the sacrament of the Lord's Supper at Buffaloe, and gave as his excuse or reason, an account, which he had by such testimony as he judged sufficient for him to proceed upon, that Mr. Campbel had publicly taught the opinions expressed in the two following propositions, viz.: 'That there is an appropriation of Christ to ourselves in the essence of saving faith, such appropriation belonging to a high degree of that faith; and that we have nothing but human authority or agreement for confessions of faith, testimonies, covenanting and fast days before the dispensation of the Lord's Supper', and as Mr. Anderson judged that these propositions were inconsistent with some articles of our testimony, it appeared upon consideration most proper not to join with Mr. Campbel in the communion till the matter should be enquired into. After some conversation on this subject, it was agreed to put this question, Whether upon supposition that the testimony upon which Mr. Anderson proceeded was sufficient, his conduct in declining to fulfill his appointment was excusable? Which question being put, was carried in the affirmative." Continuing the quotation from page 124: "It was then agreed to enquire what testimony Mr. Anderson proceeded upon; and the testimony of Mr. Wilson, a member of this court, declaring that he heard Mr. Campbel utter the aforesaid propositions in his public discourses at a late sacramental occasion at Cannamaugh,* having been produced, the question was proposed, Whether this testimony was sufficient for Mr. Anderson to proceed upon in declining to fulfill his appointment? It was carried that it was sufficient. Upon which Anderson's excuse was admitted.''

In four months' time, he, who had served for several years in the ministry with signal success in Ireland without any intimation either secret or open of heresy, had in America become a heretic, unworthy of having his fellow Seceder ministers assist him "on sacramental occasions." Thomas Campbell, without his full library and depending mainly on his Bible, might have changed doctrinally; but it would seem that the Seceder ministers of the Chartiers Presbytery were less liberal than their Old World Irish brethren. Mr. Campbell had in his parish at Ahorey used the privilege of "occasional hearing," and at night, after his services, had attended meetings in the Independent Church. He had heard some of the great figures of English and Irish Independency, such as Rowland

---

*Name of an Associate Church in Indiana County, established in 1798. It is spelled in Chartiers Pres. Minutes Cannamagh, Cannamaugh and Conemaugh. Ebenezer was the post office. This is referred to in Richardson's *Memoirs* as "up the Allegheny River" (Vol. I., p. 224). The trip there was probably made by canal boat, which required two or three days.

Hill, James Alexander Haldane, Alexander Carson (on the way to becoming an Independent), and John Walker. He had heard much about the Methodism of that day. He had an opportunity to learn of the teachings of John Glas and Robert Sandeman. He had become a member of a missionary society called the Evangelical Society, which sent out many liberal and earnest preachers to convene and preach to the general public (Richardson's *Memoirs*, Vol. I., pp. 59ff.). Just how much this "hearing" had affected Mr. Campbell's religious convictions we can not determine. He had been a great reader and student, and it may be that almost unconsciously he had grown out of the teachings and practices of the Seceder testimony.

To return to the meeting of Presbytery at Mt. Hope: At the morning session on the following day, October 28, after the reading of the minutes, Mr. Campbell made a motion which received a second, "To reconsider what respected Mr. Anderson's excuse for not fulfilling his appointment at Buffaloe." The motion was lost. "Upon which Mr. Campbel gave in a verbal protest and having said that he would not sit any longer in this Presbytery, he withdrew. It was agreed not to admit his protest, as it was without any appeal to an higher court."

Presbytery continued another day at the Mt. Hope Meeting-house (October 29). "The Presbytery entered upon the consideration of the case of Mr. Campbel, who according to Mr. Wilson's testimony had taught the erroneous tenets previously mentioned. Agreed to appoint Messrs. Anderson, Wilson, Alison and Ramsay, ministers, with John Hay ruling elder, as a committee to enquire into reports concerning erroneous opinions said to be delivered by the Rev'd Mr. Campbel, and if they judge it necessary to state the charges that appear to lie against him in the form of Libel, and in the meantime, agree not to give him any appointments on account of his disorder by leaving Presbytery.* While the members of Presbytery were attending to this business, they received a letter from Mr. Campbel containing among other things a Protest, which could not be received for the same reason as before." Messrs. Ramsay and Anderson, by appointment, drafted a reply to this letter, which was approved by Presbytery, and sent to Mr. Campbell.

We are entirely in the dark as to the contents of that letter. There is no response to our curiosity. Leaving Mr. Campbell without appointments for the next two months, deprived him of income that had been fixed by the Presbytery on July 1, 1807: "The vacancies shall give ministers that are sent to them by this Presbytery, four dollars for a sabbath and two dollars for a working-day." In all probability it gave some occasion, for the seventh

---

*Here appears in the "Minutes of Chartiers Presbytery" at page 129 a page cut out of the minute book, showing signs of having been written on to about the middle. Only a few parts of words or short words that begin the line can be read. Moreover, this writing remaining on the margin is in distinctly different handwriting than that of page 129. Might this which was removed have been the draft of the letter which was ordered sent to Mr. Campbell?

article of the Libel, which was framed by the committee, as we shall see later.

The original document corrects the only account of this Libel which is current among those who are interested in Thomas Campbell and the plan for Christian union which he gave forth to the world in 1809. Dr. Richardson, in *Memoirs of Alexander Campbell* (Vol. I., p. 224), places all responsibility for the charges against Father Campbell upon the shoulders of "a young minister, a Mr. Wilson," who "Felt it his duty, therefore, at the next meeting of the Presbytery, to lay the case before it, in the usual form of 'Libel,' containing various formal and specified charges." As shown before from the Chartiers Presbytery Minutes, a committee of four ministers and one ruling elder was charged with the duty of bringing in the Libel, if they should find it necessary. It is of interest to know somewhat about those four ministers. The Rev. Mr. Anderson (John) had become a D.D., and the Professor of Theology for the Associated Churches in the Presbytery of Chartiers on Apr. 21, 1794. He was small of stature, had the appearance of scarcely having any neck; his voice was weak, and before coming to America Mr. Anderson had found it hard to get a hearing. He was ordained in Philadelphia *sine titulo,* and itinerated for some time. In 1792 he was installed as pastor at Mill Creek and Harmon's Creek, in Beaver County in the Chartiers Presbytery. Dr. Anderson wrote in 1793 *"The Appropriation Which Is in the Nature of Saving Faith."* He lectured every day of his seminary session from three to four hours at a time. "He was in temper somewhat irascible, although distinguished for meekness and humility, and was very impatient of contradiction, so far as related to matters of principle" (*Manual of United Presbyterian Church*, p. 201). The Rev. Mr. Wilson (William), born 1770, had his literary training in Glasgow; came to America in 1791 or 1792. He was the first theological student of Dr. Anderson, mentioned above, at Harmon's Creek (now Service) in a little log house which was the seminary. He was ordained in 1800 and served at Monteurs, Flaugherty's Run and Noblestown (p. 652 in *Manual*). Mr. Allison (Thomas), was born in 1771, educated at Canonsburg Academy, studied theology with Dr. Anderson at Harmon's Run, licensed in 1800. He was ordained over Mt. Hope and Cross Creek (Va.) Churches in 1802 (*Manual*, p. 198). The Rev. Mr. Ramsay (James) was born in 1771, came from the Presbyterian Church into the Associate Churches at Frankfort, Beaver County. He studied classics under his pastor, Dr. Anderson; then went to Canonsburg Academy and later returned to take theological studies under Dr. Anderson. Mr. Ramsay was licensed to preach in 1803, and was ordained pastor of Chartiers Church in 1805. It will be seen that the committee could be of one mind, if the influence and training of a single professor remained long with his students.

Chartiers Presbytery assembled at Monteur's Run Meeting-house, Jan. 5, 1808 (the secretary wrote 1807 and some one later put in the proper year). Mr. Campbell's name is among those who are listed as present. "The minutes of the former meeting being read, Mr. Campbel offered as correction of that minute with regard to the motion he made at that meeting for the Presbytery's reconsidering their decision concerning Mr. Anderson's not fulfilling his appointment at Buffaloe; that it ought to have as a distinct motion that he should have leave to state his grievances to this Presbytery." But Presbytery refused the correction, holding "that Mr. Campbel made only one motion at the time, not two."

In the evening of the next day at a meeting in the home of Mr. Hay, it was "agreed to receive the report of the committee appointed to make enquiry concerning erroneous tenets said to have been taught publickly by Mr. Campbel." Upon which a Libel was produced, the tenor whereof follows:*

"1. It is erroneous and contrary to the Holy Scriptures or our subordinate standards to teach that a person's appropriation of Christ to himself as his own Savior, does not belong to the essence of Saving Faith; but only to a high degree of it. 1 Cor. XV. 3: 'I delivered unto you first of all that which I also received how that Christ died for our sins according to the scriptures'—compared with v. 11, 'so we preach and so ye also believed.' Ps. XXXI. 14: 'I trusted in thee, O Lord, I said thou art my God.' Acts V. 11: 'We believe that through

* The text of the Libel is written in the minutes in a very fine and sometimes ornate hand, seemingly other than the secretary's. The Libel begins on page 132, "Minutes of Chartiers Presbytery."

the grace of the Lord Jesus Christ we shall be saved.'

"Larger Catechism, Quest. 72: Justifying Faith is a saving grace whereby a sinner assenteth not only to the truth of the promise of the Gospel: but receiveth and resteth upon Christ and his righteousness therein held forth for the pardon or sin; and for the accepting and accounting his person righteous in the sight of God for salvation.

"Declaration and Testimony, Part II., Art. XIII., Sec. 6: We testify against all who deny that any persuasion, assurance or confidence that we in particular thro' the grace of our Lord Jesus Christ shall be saved, belongs to the nature of saving faith.

"But you, the Rev'd Thomas Campbell, have publickly taught this error at Conemaugh and Mt. Pleasant. Witnesses: Rev'd Wm. Wilson, Alex'r Murray, student in divinity, Patrick Douglas.

"2. It is erroneous or contrary to the Holy Scriptures and our subordinate standards to assert that a church has no divine warrant for holding Confessions of Faith as terms of communion.

"[Quotation*: (1) Scriptures, 2 Tim. 1:13; Acts 16:4; Jude 3. (2) Confession, Chap. 31, Sec. 3. (3) Declaration and Testimony, Art. 4, Sec. 1.]

"But you, the Rev'd Thomas Campbell, taught this error at Conemaugh and Buffaloe. Witnesses:

---

*From this item of the Libel unto the close, for the sake of brevity, only the sources from which citations are made will be given.

Rev'd Wm. Wilson, James Brownlee, Hugh Allison, Wm. Brownlee.

"3. It is erroneous or contrary to the Holy Scriptures and our subordinate standard to assert that it is the duty of ruling elders to pray and exhort publickly in vacant congregations.

"[Quotations: (1) Scriptures, 1 Tim. 4:13, 14; 1 Tim. 4:17; Heb. 5:4. (2) Westminster Confession in 'Office of Pastor.' (3) Larger Catechism, Question 158].

"But you, the Rev'd Thomas Campbell, taught the above error at Buffaloe. Witnesses: James Brownlee, Walter Maxwell, Hugh Allison.

"4. It is erroneous or contrary to the Holy Scriptures and our subordinate standards to assert that it is warrantable for the people of our communion to hear ministers that are in a stated opposition to our testimony (that is to the truths of God's word for which that Testimony is maintained).

"[Quotations: (1) Scriptures, Prov. 19:27; Rom. 16; Heb. 11:23; 2 John 10. (2) Larger Catechism, Ques. 108. (3) Declaration and Testimony, Part 3, Art. 1.]

"But you, the Rev'd Thomas Campbell, have publickly taught this error in Buffaloe. Witnesses, Joseph Panter, Joseph Clark, Peter Robinson, John Buchanan, Jacob Donaldson.

"5. It is erroneous or contrary to the Holy Scripture and our subordinate standards to assert that our Lord Jesus Christ was not subject to the precept as well as the penalty of the law in the stead of his people or as their surety.

"[Quotations: (1) Scriptures, Gal. 4:4; Mat. 3:5; 5:7. (2) Confession of Faith, Ch. 8, sec. 4. (3) Declaration and Testimony, Part 2, Art. 7, Sec. 1, Sec. 3.]

"But you, the Rev'd Thomas Campbell, have publickly taught the above mentioned error in Buffaloe. Witnesses: James Brownlee, Walter Maxwell, Jesse Mitchell, Hugh Allison.

"6. It is erroneous or contrary to the Holy Scriptures and our subordinate standards to assert that any man is able in this life to live without sin in thought, word and deed.

"[Quotations: (1) Scriptures, Eccle. 7:20; 1 John 1:8; Gal. 5:17. (2) Shorter Catechism, Ques. 82. (3) Declaration and Testimony, Part 2, Art. 19.]

"But you, Rev'd Thomas Campbell, have publickly taught the above mentioned error in Buffaloe. Witnesses: James Brownlee, Elizabeth Hannah.

"7. It is contrary to the Holy Scriptures and to the Rules of Presbyterial Church Government, for a minister of our communion to preach in a congregation where any of our ministers are settled, without any regular call or appointment.

"There are two ways in which an ordinary minister of the word has a regular call to exercise his office in any congregation. One is when he is sent by a Presbytery to continue for a short time (Acts 8:14). The other is when a minister is ordained the fixed pastor of a congregation (Acts 14:23).

"[Quotations: Scriptures, 1 Cor. 14:32, 33; 16:17.]

"This practice is contrary to the engagement ministers come under at their ordination to endeavor to maintain the spiritual unity and peace of this church, carefully avoiding every divisive cause.

"But you, the Rev'd Thomas Campbell, a member of this Presbytery, are chargeable with the above mentioned practice in preaching within the bounds of the Associate Congregations of Chartiers, where the Rev'd Mr. Ramsay is settled, without any regular call or appointment." (End of the Libel.)

"The several articles were read and judged relevant. After hearing Mr. Campbell on each of these articles, and also reasoning of members, it was agreed to put the Libel into Mr. Campbell's hand; which was done accordingly; and the further prosecution of this affair was delayed until the next meeting, which was appointed to be at Buffaloe on the 2d Tuesday of February next. At which meeting though the Presbytery did not appoint a formal trial, nor summon witnesses; yet they are resolved as far as the parties agree, to make use of the testimony of such witnesses as may be present as well as of reasoning on the several articles of the Libel, in order to bring the affair to an issue at that meeting." ("Minutes Chartiers Presbytery," p. 137.)

The *Manual of the United Presbyterian Church* (p. 266) is in error in the following sentence: "And at the next meeting tried Mr. Campbell for error in doctrine in seven different particulars, found him guilty and suspended him." It was not the next meeting after the charge of heresy, for that was occupied with hearing the report of the committee and appointing a next meeting as the above dates show. Moreover, the sentence cited seems to convey the idea that he was found guilty on all charges, which was not the case.

Chapter III

PRESBYTERY UPHOLDS HERESY LIBEL

PRESBYTERY met at the Buffaloe Meetinghouse on Feb. 9, 1808. "Mr. Campbell requested the Presb'y to define more particularly the method in which they were to proceed in his case. It was agreed that the method of procedure was sufficiently determinate as stated in the minutes of the last meeting; & they resolved to proceed accordingly, & to enter upon that business at the beginning of the next sederunt. It having been moved that as the Presb'y had been invited by Mr. Anderson, of Buffaloe, to go to his meeting-house, or on the inclemency of the weather, it was agreed to adjourn to meet there at 10 o'clock to-morrow." ("Minutes Chartiers Presbytery," p. 138.)

Here the minute book bears mute testimony to a mysterious transaction, which will probably never be revealed. The legend reads: "Mr. Anderson's meeting-house, Feb. 10." Following occur minutes about one-third of a page, written in the same hand as those of February 9, crossed out. Pages 139, 140 and 141 are other paper, roughly cut and sewed into the book and contain minutes in another handwriting, while page 142 is blank. Arriving at page 143, there is the same writing as on page 138 and the crossing out in the same fashion. It is useless to speculate upon this strange discovery. Coming to page 139, the record reads: "Mr. Anderson's meeting house, Feb. 10.

"The Presbytery met and constituted with prayer by the Moderator. Sederunt as before. Agreed to enter upon the consideration of the several articles of charge against Mr. Campbel. It was judged proper to hear Mr. Campbel's answer to each of these articles—accordingly they were read one by one, and Mr. Campbel's answer to each of them was heard distinctly.

"To the first article his answer was, 'With respect to faith I believe that the soul of man is the subject of it; the Divine Spirit is the author of it; the Divine Word the rule and reason of it; Christ, and him crucified the object of it; the Divine pardon, acceptance and assistance, or grace here and glory hereafter, the direct, proper and formal end of it. That it is an act of the whole soul intensively looking to, embracing and leaning upon Jesus Christ for complete salvation—for with the heart man believeth unto righteousness—that it is the right of all that hear the gospel so to believe upon the bare declaration, invitation and promise of God, holden forth equally and indiscriminately unto all that hear it, without restriction or exception of any kind; though at the same time none can do this, except it be given him of God. That as the habit, power or principle of faith divinely wrought in the soul by the word and spirit of God is increased and strengthened, growing up in many to a full assurance of eternal life, even in the direct actings of a vigorous and lively faith. But that this faith may be in lower degrees of it where the assurance is not; that therefore this assurance can not be of the essence of faith: for if it were, then none that had true faith, could be possibly without it.'"

After some conversation on this answer, it was agreed to put the following question to him: Whether he agreed to the article of the Declaration and Testimony concerning the appropriation of saving faith and the terms there used on that subject? and whether he considered those ministers who testified against the act of General Assembly of the Church in Scotland in 1720, condemning the doctrine of the Marrow* concerning the appropriation of faith, as maintaining the cause of God and truth? This question accordingly put, he refused to give a positive answer because he considered this question as insinuating that he was receding from the testimony to which he had professed adherence.

"To the 2d article his answer was: 'With respect to Confessions of Faith and Testimonies I believe that the church has all the Divine warrant for such exhibitions of the truth, that our Confession and Testimony adduce for that purpose; and that it is lawful and warrantable to use them as terms of communion insofar as our testimony requires; in which sense I have never opposed them.' Being dealt with as to what he meant by saying in the former meeting at Monture's Run 'that we have neither precept nor example in Scripture for

---

*A book reprinted at Edinburgh in 1718, entitled "The Marrow of Modern Divinity."

Confessions of Faith and Testimonies,' he answered 'that there was no formal nor express precept to that purpose.' The question put, Whether the Presbytery was satisfied with Mr. Campbel's written answers to the first and second articles, or not; it was carried in the negative.

"To the third article his answer was, 'With respect to Elders, it appears to me that it is their duty as the ordained overseers and rulers of the house of God to see that all his ordinances be duly observed by those over whom the Holy Ghost hath made them overseers; and that, of course, in the absence or want of the teaching elder, the others should do what is competent to them to prevent the objects of their charge from forsaking the assembling of themselves together; but should for this purpose meet with them in the usual place of their assembling, read the word, make prayer and sing the praises of God, catechise the young and exhort all to the due and faithful performance of their duties according to the word of God.'

"And to the fourth article his answer was, 'I believe that in the present broken and divided state of the church, when Christians have not an opportunity of hearing those of their own party, it is lawful for them to hear other ministers preach the gospel where the publick worship is not corrupted with matters of human invention.' After some reasoning, the Presbytery found that Mr. Campbel holds in his answers to the 2d and 3rd articles of the Libel the tenets with which he is charged in these articles.

"To the 5th article his answer was, 'That our Lord Jesus Christ was subject both to the precept and penalty of the law for his people; that if he had not been subject to the former he could not have been subject to the latter as their surety: and that by his one obedience unto the death he hath wrought out for them a complete deliverance from the curse of the law, being made a curse for them; which obedience is embraced and rested upon by all that believe for their justification; and is actually imputed to them for righteousness, as if they had wrought it out in their own persons.' After some explanation, the Presbytery admitted his declaration in answer to the 5th article to be satisfactory as to that point of doctrine.

"To the 6th article ("Minutes Chartiers Presbytery," p. 141) his answer was, 'I believe that no mere man since the fall, is able in this life to keep the commandments of God, but doth daily break them in thought, word or deed, either by actual transgression or want of conformity in some degree or other; and that our very best actions are so imperfect that they could not be acceptable to God without a Mediator. These are my sentiments respecting the matters alleged against me, and which I constantly believe and teach. Thomas Campbel.' "

It would seem that Mr. Campbell had read from a paper his answers, and that the paper was handed in at the end of the reading of the sixth article. Or it might be that reference is made to the sixth article alone. The minutes proceed:

"The doctrine expressed in his answer was approved in general; but not his criticism on the answer to the 82nd Question of the Shorter Catechism, putting the word *or* instead of *and;* so far as it seems to imply that a man may be free from sin either in his thoughts, or in his words or in his actions.

"To the 7th article his answer was, 'As to the 7th charge, I acknowledge that I preached at Cannonsburg, but not in a congregation where any of our ministers is settled, nor yet without a regular call, as I conceive I have appointment to preach the gospel and the call of some of the most regular and respectable people of that vicinity to preach, thereof which I can produce sufficient testimonials if required. Thomas Campbel.'

"This answer was not admitted as satisfactory. Adjourned to meet to-morrow at Buffaloe Meeting-house. Closed with prayer."

Now on page 143 begins the paging of the book proper.

"Buffaloe Meeting-house, Feb. 10, a. m., 1808.

"The Presbytery met and constituted with prayer by the Mod'r; sederunt as before. . . . Mr. Campbell gave in a declaration with regard to the 2nd article, a paper containing the following words on the one side, 'That we have no formal or express command either by Christ or his apostles enjoining upon the Pastors of the Catholic Church or any part of it to draw up a compend of the Divine truths contained in the word of God and to make the approbation of them a term of communion to entrants into the Church of Christ as a *sine qua non* of their admission.' Signed Tho's Campbell. [The name by the secretary with a double "l".] Containing the following words on the other side, 'This I alledged at Monteur's Run when discussing the relevancy of the Libel upon the 2nd article of charge, which I denied and was not defending, but only supposing that any person who might have uttered such a sentiment might mean no more that [than?] what I offered as probable in that case.' Signed: Tho's Campbell. With regard to the 5th article Mr. Campbell objected to the word *explanation* in the minute, and insisted that his answers should be what he had given in writing; upon which Mr. C. was asked whether he would admit the words 'as a covenant of works' to be added as an explanation to the word 'law' in his answer; he answered peremptorily in the negative.

"The Presbytery agreed to the calling of witnesses in support of the charge: The witnesses in the first article the Rev'd Mr. Wilson, Mr. Silcock, Mr. Murray were sworn.

"Mr. Silcock deposed he heard Mr. C. at Mt. Pleasant in discourse on the subject of saving faith: He opposed what some divines allege the nature of saving faith to consist in: He said it was not a persuasion that Christ is mine or ours; that they might believe this without being the subject of saving grace; and warned his hearers of supposing faith to consist in that: And also that it did not consist in believing certain propositions, but in believing or embracing the person of Christ; and alluded to the definition in the Shorter Catechism, 'Receiving and resting in Christ.'

"Being asked whether he represented that definition as one of the best that we can give of saving faith? An. I believe he did. Question: Was what he delivered opposite to what is contained in our testimony. An. He was not certain. Q. Did Mr. C. mention the Testimony? An. No. Q. Did he speak of appropriation as belonging to a high degree of faith? An. He did not.

"Mr. Murray deposed he heard Mr. Campbell preaching at Mt. Pleasant. He said as nearly as I can recollect, The definition of saving faith as consisting in an appropriation of Christ as mine in the offer of the gospel is not a good one; the definition given in the W. M. Catechism Confession or Catechism (he does not know which) was much better. Being asked whether Mr. C. gave any reason why the above mentioned definition was not a good one; answered, he spoke at some length on it in showing that the definition of the W. Assembly was better. Question. Did he use the word 'appropriation'? Ans. He could not be positive. Question. Did he represent the appropriation of Christ as mine as belonging, not to the nature, but to a high degree of faith? An. Not. Q. Whether he had an impression of his combating the doctrine of the appropriation of faith, or that each appro'n was not in the direct act of faith, or that each appro'n was not in the direct act of faith? An. He could not say.

"Mr. Wilson deposed, that on the Friday before the disp'n of the L. S. he, i. e., Mr. C. faulted the phrase which is commonly made use of, viz.: appro'n in the definition of saving faith; and wished that they had rested satisfied with the form of sound words in our S. Catechism, a receiving and resting. Then in my judgment, he explained our views of the appro'n of saving faith into sensible assurance. Between sermons I said to Mr. C. I was sorry that from some expressions he had dropt, the people would be ready to conjecture that he denied there was an appropriation belonging to the nature of saving faith. Mr. C. answered, Did I say so? On Saturday I endeavored to show that there is an appropriation belonging to the nature of saving and justifying faith. After sermon, Mr. C., in his address to the people, wished that he might not be misunderstood; he did not deny that there is an appro'n and persuasion belonging to faith; but an appro'n and persuasion did not belong to the nature of saving and justifying faith, but to a high degree of strong faith: and then, in my judgment, explained his views of a high degree of a strong faith into that of the assurance of sense.

"The witness being asked whether he heard Mr. C. utter the proposition contained in the Libel in *ipsissimis verbis,* assured, not in *ipsissimis verbis,* but to the amount in his judgment. Being asked, When he said he was sorry for what Mr. C. had said, answered, In a little house before Judge Smith's door.

"Witnesses called by (John McElroy deposed Mr. C. (that Mr. C. treating of the (nature of faith, mentioned that in his country there were several ideas with respect to faith: some conceived that it consisted in believing that Christ was theirs and he was theirs: which definition he did not apprehend to be just: He alluded to the S. C. receiving and resting on Christ for salv'n, &c.: He added, that to him faith was pleasingly defined in Heb. XI:1—"Being asked whether he knew whose views of faith Mr. C. was opposing; answered, he did not: But Mr. C. said, Faith did not consist in names or sounds, but in substance.

"James McElroy deposed, he heard Mr. C. preach on Rom. XII:5. Speaking of faith as nearly as I can recollect, he said, The word of God was the rule of faith; and the mercy of God in the free offer and promises of the gospel was the ground and warrant why we should believe. He was not positive as to the expressions used by Mr. C. A definition that he gave of faith was in 1 Ep. of John, 'He that believeth that Jesus is the Christ is born of God:' that these words might be used in a reciprocal manner as meaning either that he who was born of God believed that Jesus is the Christ: or he that believeth, &c. But here said he you may mistake; it is not merely the number of letters in the name of Christ, but in apprehending him to be the character typified, prophesied and promised under the O. T. the co-essential and co-eternal Son of God. But he found his idea happily and completely expressed in the S. C. receiving and resting, &c. But said that he could not help remarking in the opinion of some who say 'that we might believe that Christ died for us in particular; that he is our Savior; and that we shall be saved through him.' For my own part, said he, I rest completely satisfied in the definition in 1 Ep. of John. He s'd Faith did not consist in logical propositions, deductions of human science or syllogisms of the brain, but in the substantial realities of the understanding and heart. Being asked whether Mr. C. used the word appropriation, answered, he did not. Asked whether he used the terms in the 1st article of the Libel; an'd, Not to the best of his recollection.

"Entered upon the 2d article. Witnesses Hugh Allison, Rev'd Wm. Wilson, Jas. Brownlee, Wm. Brownlee. Mr. C. objected to H. A. that he had been in the habit of hurting characters: But the objection was deemed to be unfounded.

"Mr. Wilson deposed that on Sab. at Conemaugh sacrament at the usual time of fencing the table, Mr. C. observed that on former occasions they had heard the precepts of the moral law gone over in setting a fence about the table; but this he considered as unnecessary; therefore he would propose our terms of communion: 1st. The Scriptures; and that where there was a plain precept, that he who runs might read. 2d. The Westmin. Confession of faith; and this not particularly but generally; as there were many things that were not proven, & others that could not be agreed to; and those mentioned that concerning the magistrates' power. 3d. A testimony: but this not particularly, but generally; for to require it as a particular term of communion would be to require an implicit faith. On Monday Mr. C. observed to the people that he begged they would bear with him, as he would now come nearer home: He said the church maintained many things that they had only human authority for; such were a Confession of faith & a Testimony: Those who had not a Confession of faith and yet did the same things that we did, were nothing the worse because they had not them; and we are nothing the better because we have them. He s'd was he cast in a land where there were none but Lutherans he could freely join them, provided they would allow him to maintain his own principles; but the moment they required an assent of him to theirs, he could not join them. Being asked what reason Mr. C. [had] for not fencing the table, answered because of the care that was taken by the session in not admitting such gross characters. Being asked whether Mr. C. said that he would not go over the commands, or only those gross characters; ans'd, Mr. C. declined going over the commands and did not do so; but mentioned these gross characters. Being asked whether Mr. C. delivered the thing, related by the Deponent in the words now used, ans'd in the words or to the amount. Being asked whether Mr. C. uttered the opinion charged against him in the terms of the libel, ans'd as above; Mr. C. said the church has many things for which they had only human authority, such was a confession of faith and testimony. The Deponent s'd Mr. C. declared that it cannot be expected that in the present state of the church all the members should be of one opinion; therefore Luther and Calvin [whose error —deponent's or Mr. C's—in using Calvin instead of Zwingli?] should not have separated, as it was a mere opinion about consubstantiation, which they themselves did not understand: and that ministers had done more hurt to the church by their opinions than ever they did good; for when an opinion is once embraced, they cannot think of dropping it; witness the division which took place among ourselves respecting the Burghers-oath which those who were opposed to it would be willing to give up with, if they could in decency; and along this line he s'd if they could give it a decent burial.

"Adjourned to meet to-morrow at ten o'clock. Closed with prayer."

[Page 146.] "Buffaloe, Feb. 11, 10 o'clock a. m. "Opened sederunt as before. Proceeded to receive the testimony of witnesses. H. Allison deposed that he heard Mr. C. preaching at Buffaloe, when he said that confessions and testimonies should not be made terms of communion; because young people wanting admission into the church could not understand the twentieth part of them: he thinks he said the Scriptures should be the only rule, especially the N. T.—Being asked how this was introduced, ans'd, That it was by way of exhortation in the evening as far as he remembers. Being asked whether he heard Mr. C. assert as in the terms of the libel; answered, Not in the terms, but as he has answered above. Being asked whether Mr. C. said, "The rule of faith and practices or the rule of admission"; ans'd, he thinks 'Admission', but is not positive. Being asked whether Mr. C. said the 20th part, or some parts; ans'd, he is positive that he used either that or some such part. Being asked whether the words as to Testimonies and Confessions not being terms of communion, were Mr. C's words, or only his opinion of the amount of his words, ans'd, that they were his words.

"Witnesses)

by Mr. C.) John Wilkins deposed he heard him often on that subject. One time I heard him say, That human composure was the greatest hurt [?] to the church that ever it met with: One doctor after another brought rules into the church which became a form and was the cause of great rents and divisions in the church. If people were to go over these human composures and take the word of God for the only rule it would be the likeliest way to bring about unanimity or peace in the church. [End of page 146.] He added, Not that I have anything against confessions, creeds or testimonies: for they are laudable and praiseworthy, and I believe done with a good design; or words to that import. Preaching in the school house the sab. evening, after showing the love of God to the church, and how much they had deviated from the apostolic church, he showed that we had fallen from the love of our ancestors at the time of the Reformation; then he showed how much they had done; and how they had given testimonies and had suffered for the truth; and how little zeal we showed for the truth which seemed to show that we had lost our first love; that we had as good a right to stand for the truth as our forefathers had; that we were bound to do so; for the church of Christ is still one; notwithstanding we were not in being when the cov'ts were made. Being asked what he understood Mr. C. meant by human composures that had done hurt to the church, ans'd, he thought that one thing he meant was Wall's imitation of the Psalms. Being asked whether he ever heard Mr. C. say that confessions and testimonies should not be terms of communion, ans'd, he did not remember. Being asked whether what he deposed was in the very words of Mr. C. or to this import, ans'd, it was to this amount.

"Nathaniel Robinson deposed, that he heard Mr. C. preach in Buff., Washington and Mt. Pleasant. At Buff. I heard him one day say concerning acts and testimonies that he did not approve putting them in the place of Holy Scripture, citing a passage in Deut. VI. that we should teach our children, &c. Another day at Washington he mentioned acts & testimonies and confessions of faith, alluding to the same doctrine. He addressed them thus: Brethren, I wish you not to mistake me here that I should be thought to disapprove of creeds or confessions or acts or testimonies, for I approve of them as much as any, only use them in their own proper place; for I think they are an excellent help for the strengthening of our faith. Being asked whether Mr. C. disapproved of acts and testimonies in any sense, answered, he disapproved of putting them in place of Scriptures or out of the proper place. Being asked whether Mr. C. showed what it was to put them in place of the Scripture, or any abuse of the confessions or testimonies, ans'd, Mr. C. said afterward Confessions and Testimonies were abused in the manner of joining with somebody, particularly when they were presented to young people, for their assent when they did not understand them; or to that amount. Being asked whether he ever heard Mr. C. say that creeds and confessions should not be used as terms of communion, ans'd that he did not hear him say so. Being asked whether Mr. C. [said] that the presenting of a confession or testimony to ignorant in order to their admission tended to lead them into an implicit faith, ans'd, that he did.

"James McElroy deposed that Mr. C. preaching in Math. XXVIII. 19 at Buffaloe taught that the O. T. church had nothing but the O. T. for its instruction & direction & did not complain for the want of anything else. Then Mr. C. showed that the N. T. was the foundation of the N. T. church, as the O. T. was of the old: That in obedience to this command given by Christ to his apostles they were either faithful or unfaithful; that they were faithful all would concur with him in the affirmative, & that if Moses was faithful as a servant over his house, much more was Christ over his own house: and that it was evident from the command given that he who commanded had enjoined no other but what he had engaged to give them sufficient strength to perform. And then drew the conclusion that they had accomplished everything that was commanded them: and therefore the Scriptures of the O. & N. T. were a sufficient rule to the church for her faith and conduct. (Mr. C. spoke to this effect.) And that then speaking in allusion to confessions and testimonies said that human systems might be and had been edifying and useful to the church; but the great disadvantage or danger was that persons ever having imbibed an opinion might be too tenacious of it & that numerous examples might teach us that it is much easier to learn a thing than unlearn it, when once learned. Then speaking of testimonies and confessions, he said they were and had been edifying to the church; but it was one disadvantage in the manner in which they were received, that persons coming for communion with the church were not sufficiently acquainted with them: It was not infrequent for a youth of 17, making application for admission to the church, who, when examined, manifested that he had no knowledge of them at all. But Mr. C. was sorry to find that not only persons of that age, but events often find a boy of 70 was not acquainted with them, and that there was danger here of too much implicit faith: that if persons who were concerned in their admission would take pains sufficiently to instruct them, and see that they had a completent knowledge of these things, that would wholly come up to the spirit or reason of them: but unless this method was adopted, it would be much better to forego the use of testimonies and confessions. But when Mr. C. came to speak of division and the causes of division, he said that persons might be more attentive to the human than to the divine testimony. He then mentioned confessions and testimonies as one cause of division, & that we often find more controversies originating among mankind upon confessions and testimonies than upon the word of God. Being asked whether he heard Mr. C. express himself in the terms of this article in the libel, answered, that he did not recollect. Being asked whether Mr. C. specified any article of the Confession or testimony that had been a cause of controversy, answered that Mr. C. instanced the article concerning magistrates. Being asked whether he ever heard Mr. C. inculcate the duty of the church to have a confession or testimony & to make it a term of communion, answered, that he heard him inculcate the utility of a confession and testimony; but as to its being duty to have it for a term of communion, I do not recollect to have heard him speaking. But that it was an excellent means of communicating our doctrinal ideas to one another.

[Page 148.] "John McMillen deposed, One day I heard him say, in preaching that Confessions and testimonies were either like gold or silver tried, as far as agreeable to God's word.

"Entered on the 5th article of the libel, Jesse Mitchell deposed that he heard Mr. C. on the subject, but cannot recollect a full sentence of what was then delivered, but thinks that it was the same as what is contained in the declaration given into this Presb'y by Mr. C. on this article.

"Walter Maxwell, saith he can recollect none of Mr. C.'s words, but will give in propositions which he formed in his own mind from what he heard Mr. C. say: That the moral law was not the condition of the cov't of works as made with Adam, as the representative of his posterity. That the penalty of death and the promise of life were suspended on the refraining from or eating the fruit of the forbidden tree. That Adam could not transgress in anything else. Taking these things in connection with what he after said concerning Christ's obedience, I formed the opinion that Mr. C. taught that Christ was not made subject to the precept of the law. I heard him another time; the subject Gal V:1. He then explained the same subject in nearly the same terms with those of the notes of a sermon which he read on Tuesday to this P'by, with this addition, that Christ was not made under the precept of the law to deliver his people from the obligation of conformity to it. I was led to think that what he formerly delivered was the same statement, because he said that we often read of imputed righteousness, but never of imputed holiness. Being asked whether the deponent meant that what he has declared be the words of Mr. C. or his opinion concerning the import of his words, answered that it was the latter. Being asked whether the deponent heard Mr. C. in speaking of Christ's being made under the law, represent the law as a cov't of works, ans'd, that Mr. C. as he understood him, asserted that the law of the 10 commands was not the cov't of works, but that Christ was made under the law of the 10 commands; and cited Gal. IV: 4, 5.

"Hugh Allison deposed that he heard Mr. C. say that Christ was not made under the moral law, but cannot recollect in what connection he used the expression.

"Adjourn'd to meet this evening at Robert Wylie's at 7 o'clock. Closed with prayer.

"Mr. Wylie's house, same day in the evening. [The records do not show that Mr. Campbell was present; they do not indicate either that his trial was touched upon.]"

Beginning on page 149 are the minutes of the following day's meeting which evaluated the evidence.

"Buff. Meeting-house, Feb. 12, 10 a. m., Saturday.

"The Presbytery having considered the evidence brought in support of the articles of the Libel judged the 1 & 2 clearly proved; the 5th they found not sufficiently proved, tho Mr. C's declaration on that head was not so full and satisfactory as to remove all suspicions of error. The 3rd, 4th & 7th were acknowledged in his declarations given in to Presb'y and still adhered to by him.'"*

[Here on page 150 is found the paragraph that follows with a great inclusive X over it, but with an asterisk that corresponds to the one noted above]: "Mr. Campbell objected to the Presb'y proceeding to decide upon the 1st and 2nd articles of the Libel, alleging that there might be witnesses found in Conemaugh who would prove the contrary of what Mr. Wilson had deposed concerning Mr. C's teaching there. But, this objection did not appear sufficient to sist procedure in this stage of the business for the following reasons: 1st. At the last meeting of the Presb'y it was determined to make use of the testimony of witnesses on both sides, as well as reasoning on the several articles of the Libel, as far as the parties can agree, in order to bring the affair to an issue at their next meeting; & Mr. C. concurred with the Presb'y in calling witnesses and reasoning on the articles. 2d. All the testimony he could bring from Conemaugh could only be negative, and could not overthrow what has been positively deposed. 3d. Mr. C. did not propose to prove that he had taught in Conemaugh that there is an 'appropriation in the nature of saving faith,' and that 'Confessions of Faith should be made terms of communion.' 4th. Presb'y judges that there was sufficient testimony to prove that Mr. C. has taught the errors contained in the charges, exclusively of Mr. Wilson."

On page 151 ("Minutes Chartier's Presbytery") there is record of the meeting at Mt. Hope on March 8, 1808. Mr. Campbell was present, but was not included in the list of those present. The minutes relate that the Presbytery received a remonstrance from Mr. Campbell that it should reconsider its action, and that he spoke in favor of his request. Says the record: "On motion Presbytery refused to grant request."

On page 173 there is record of a meeting at Mr. Allison's in the afternoon of March 11, 1808, a continuation of the meeting on March 8. (Two days had been spent in dealing with an issue between Jacob Donaldson and others, which resulted in his suspension from office of ruling elder.) It seems that after Mr. Campbell left the meeting and Presbytery was adjourned, it was reconstituted for the sole purpose of making Mr. Campbell's suspension "indefinite *sine die*": "The Presbytery on the first day of this meeting having heard Mr. C. read a remonstrance and having further conversation with him afterward found they could not obtain any satisfaction from him with respect to the articles of charge brought against him, continue the suspension *sine die,* which he was laid under at the last meeting. This was a part of the business of this meeting; but had been omitted until the meeting was closed. The members present agreed to constitute the Presbytery in order to transact a piece of business which, after the leaving of Mr. Campbell was intended to be done this meeting. The Presbytery appoint Mr. Allison to intimate this deed continuing Mr. Campbell's suspension in Buffaloe congregation when fulfilling his appointment there." The record shows only for this meeting "Sederunt Messrs. Anderson, Wilson and Allison"—not a very large group of the Presbytery to take such a step.

At the Presbytery meeting on Apr. 20, 1808, there was a report made by a committee which dealt with Mr. Campbell's Protest, but the substance of the report is not written into the minutes. On the succeeding day we read that an addition to the draft of answer to Mr. Campbell's protest was made and accepted. This was evidently to get the report into shape for the meeting of the Synod to which Mr. Campbell now elected to carry his case.

Chapter IV

SYNOD REVERSES PRESBYTERY IN PART

WE must turn now to the "Minutes of the Synod of the Associate Churches" to follow the fortunes of Thomas Campbell. Synod seems to have convened on May 18, 1808, in Philadelphia, and the name of Mr. Campbell is found as one of the ministers present. On the following day, May 19, as the fourth matter for the consideration of the Synod we read "Reasons of protest and appeal by Mr. Thomas Campbell against the Presb'y of Chartiers, in his case and particularly proceedings of a deed of said Presb'y suspending him from the office of the ministry, and Answer by Presb'y." As a fifth item there is listed "Petitions from Buffaloe, Chartiers, Mt. Pleasant and Burgettstown in favour of Mr. Campbell."

On May 20, which was Friday, the Synod entered upon the matter between Mr. Campbell and Chartiers Presbytery. "The Minutes of Presb'y relative thereto were read, together with a remonstrance by Mr. Campbell, given into said Presb'y. Read his reasons of protest and appeal and the Presby's answer. Adjourned. At three in the afternoon, Proceeded to read the articles of the libel upon which Mr. Campbell was tried, with his declarations relative to each article as given in the Presb'y and also the depositions of witnesses.

And all papers having been read, parties were heard. Delayed further consideration until next Sed."

Saturday, May 21: "Resumed the consideration of Mr. Campbell's cause. And agreed to proceed in the following order. 1st. To read over again the articles of the libel one by one, with Mr. Campbell's declarations relative thereto; and then consider whether the Presby's further proceedings against him might not have been obviated thereby. The first article was read and his declaration in reference to it. And after members had spoken their minds and before coming to any decision whether the declaration ought to have been rested in as satisfactory, or whether this article was proved, parties were again heard in reference to it. And after several insisting that, before proceeding further in this way, the Synod would judge of the manner in which the Presb'y entered upon and conducted the process, whether regular or not; after long conversation adjourned to meet at 9 o'clock Monday morning. Closed with prayer."

At three in the afternoon of Monday, May 23: "Resumed the consideration of Mr. Campbell's protest. And, after some conversation, resolved to read again 'Reasons of Protest and Answers Thereto,' take the judgment of Synod upon them part by part, then decide upon the articles of the libel, and afterwards, if necessary, appoint a committee to bring in an *overture* on the whole cause. And it appearing that Mr. Anderson had declined fulfilling an appointment by the Presb'y of Chartiers to dispense the Lord's Supper at Buffaloe along with Mr. Campbell because of reports he had heard concerning him of his publicly teaching principles inconsistent with our profession, and also that the Presb'y had at their meeting at Mt. Hope sustained his excuse on that ground for doing so—the Synod disapproved of Mr. A's conduct in said instance, because he had not 1st written Mr. C. on the subject, or sought an interview with him; and likewise of the Presb'y sustaining said excuse.

"The Synod next sustained the Presb'y answers to Mr. C's charge against them for denying him appointment at said meeting, and for instituting an enquiry into the truth of reports respecting him, the *fama clamosa* laying a sufficient foundation for their doing so.

"Again, it appearing to the Synod that at the meeting of Presb'y at Montour's Run in Dec. when they put the libel into Mr. Campbell's hand, an agreement had been entered into between the parties not to proceed at next meeting at Buffaloe in Feb. in the formal trial of the libel, except upon certain conditions, nor even to enter upon it, in case an accommodation of differences could be accomplished by means of free conversation; and particularly that they should not bring the trial to an issue by calling witnesses, except with consent of parties; but that, however, the Presb'y, after hearing certain witnesses on both sides, did bring the trial to an issue, without allowing the privilege he claimed of citing, or the Presby's causing to be cited, other witnesses for his exculpation, and giving him opportunity for that purpose: the Synod judged the reasons advanced by the Presb'y for bringing the trial to an issue in such circumstances insufficient. [In the minutes there were two lines crossed out and there was written into the margin words seen above; i. e., 'to be cited' —to 'for that purpose.']

"From this judgment of Synod, Messrs. Anderson & Ramsay, ministers, S. Murdoch & J. Templeton, elders, declared their dissent for reasons to be afterwards given in.

"Tuesday, May 24. The Synod met and was opened with prayer by the Mod'r. Members present as above. Read the minutes of the last sitting. Reasons of dissent, of which said minutes, were given and read and are as follows: 'We dissent from the judgment of the Synod last evening determining that the Presb'y of Chartiers acted unjustly and contrary to their agreement with Mr. Campbell at Monteur's Run in bringing his affairs to an issue at their next meeting at Buffaloe for the following reasons.' [Here follow two paragraphs in which the committee covered the issues of what the minutes of the Presbytery had allowed them to do and alleged that they had acted as they had engaged to do, and again that Presbytery was at no fault in not allowing Mr. Campbell time and opportunity to bring in witnesses from Conemaugh, for he had already been condemned by witnesses from elsewhere.] Messrs. Shaw and Bullion, together with the Moderator, were appointed a committee to present an answer to the 'Reasons of Dissent' presented by persons from Chartiers Presbytery.

"A motion was made and seconded that in consideration of the Synod's judging that the proceedings of the Presb'y of Chartiers in the trial of Mr. Campbell were in the instance specified irregular, they find it necessary to lay aside any further consideration of the trial as brought before them by his protest and appeal, that notwithstanding they highly approve of the care shown by Presb'y to check the appearance of a departure in any minister under their inspection from our received principles, yet, on the ground of the aforesaid irregularity, they reverse the sentence of suspension passed by them on Mr. C., and order a new trial, or deal with Mr. C. himself. The motion, after discussion, was adopted and the said sentence accordingly reversed. Against which deed of reversal Mr. Ramsay in his own name (and) of all who should adhere to him offered a verbal protest. He was directed to put his protest in writing, which he agreed to do. After deliberating whether they should order a new trial, or deal with Mr. C. themselves, the Synod resolved on this last. And after some conversation on the mode of proceeding, 1st to consider his written declaration on the several articles of libel given in to the Presb'y, to see whether they were satisfactory or not, and in the event of their being found not satisfactory, or found to infer censure, to determine accordingly, or otherwise to require further explanation by interrogatories. His declaration on the 1st article was read and conversed upon at considerable length. And, likewise on the 2d; after conversing on which the Synod adjourned to meet at 3 p. m.

"At 3 p. m. proceeded in reading and considering Mr. C's declarations relative to articles of libel, particularly 3rd, 4th and 6th, after which a Com. was appointed to bring in an overture expressive of the mind of the Synod in regard to the declaration read and considered, taken in connection with what Mr. C. states in his paper of 'Reasons and Protest'—Messrs. Pringle, Hamilton & McCullock to be said Com."

On Wednesday, May 25, the report of the committee was called for as to Mr. Campbell's declarations on the articles of libel, and it was given and read and considered article by article. Says the record: "With a view to some alteration in it, Synod agreed to recommit said report. Answers to reasons of dissent given in by Messrs. Anderson, &c. against a judgment of Synod: 1. It is to be observed that the dissenters have withheld a very material part of the minutes of the Presb'y of Chartiers to which they refer in their dissent and have founded their first reason of dissent upon a partial view of said minute. In the reason of dissent it is said that according to the minute, the Presb'y engaged themselves to make use of the testimony of witnesses on both sides in order to bring the affair to an issue at next meeting. But here a very important clause in the Presby's minute is altogether omitted, which is, 'that they were to proceed only so far as the parties agree.' Now in a subsequent page of the Presby's book it is declared that Mr. Campbell objected to the Presby's proceeding to decide upon the articles of libel, because there might be witnesses found who would prove the contrary of what Mr. Wilson had deposed concerning Mr. C. The fact then is what Mr. C. stated to the Synod; namely, that he did not consent to the trial being issued at the meeting of Presb'y at Buffaloe, alluded to, and the dissenters are doing injustice to Synod in blaming them for proceeding according to Mr. C's assertions, as it plainly appears from the book of Presby's records, that he asserted nothing but what was well warranted by the Presby's minutes. 2. It seems strange that the dissenters should object as they do in the 1st part of their 2d reason to a sentence of Synod, sustaining an objection to Mr. C's to the Presby's procedure, when the minutes of Presb'y bears clearly that the trial was to proceed only as far as parties could agree. In consistency with their own resolution, the Presb'y were bound to stop proceedings at that time, if Mr. C. was pleased to object, and yet the P'b'y blame a sentence of Synod containing an objection which the P'b'y themselves ought to have sustained, according to previous agreement. But putting affair of mutual consent out of the question, we reckon an adherence to judicial forms of process essential to the obtaining of justice, necessary for maintaining the honor and authority of the court, for preventing all contest about the validity of its sentence, and that the accused may not have any pretext whatever for alledging that they have been cruelly or unjustly treated.

"It is immaterial in point of right whether what Mr. C. was to produce was positive or not. Exculpatory evidence, we presume, ought in no case, to be precluded, and in ordinary cases, is the first evidence that ought to be completely heard according to form of process. Wherefore although it were granted to the Dissenters that the accusations were sufficiently proven, yet as the P'b'y had not appointed a formal trial to take place at Buffaloe, as Mr. C. objected and alledged that he was grievously injured, by not allowing him the legal time to produce witnesses, which, he said, might be found to prove the contrary of what the witnesses on the part of P'b'y testified against him, and as it is possible that the witnesses Mr. C. proposed to bring might, if not totally, yet partially have exculpated, and so lessened the degree of criminality, we can not but think that the P'b'y withheld from him those rights to which he had a just claim, and those means of clearing himself, which every court of justice, more especially an ecclesiastical court, ought always to grant to the accused. The Synod therefore do not seem to have proceeded, as the dissenters alledge, upon a mere pretense, but to have been actuated by a desire to support their character as a Court of Christ, for justice, honour and impartiality and so impress upon the mind of the accused a sense of the purpose of Synod to do justice between him and the P'b'y of Chartiers, freely blaming wherever they found cause."

"Minutes of Associate Synod" for May 26: "The Com. appointed on Mr. Campbell's affair gave in their report which was read, and, after discussion adopted as follows:

" '1st article contains a charge that Mr. C. affirms that a person's appropriation of Christ to himself as his own Saviour does not belong to the essence of saving faith.' In the judgment of the Com. there are strong grounds to conclude that Mr. C. does not believe in the appropriation or assurance of faith, at least in the sense in which the term is used by the Associate Church. For (1) in his written declaration on this subject to the P'b'y of Chartiers in which it was his design to give satisfaction on this head, he declines giving that description of justifying and saving faith which he knew would be a full vindication of himself against the charge; for Mr. C. in saying that faith 'is a looking to, embracing and leaning upon Christ for salvation,' says nothing more than those would affirm concerning it, who deny the doctrine of appropriation. Besides the same thing may be concluded from a clause in Mr. C.'s Reasons of Protest where he affirms that to believe that Christ shed his blood for us in particular, and that we in particular shall be saved through him, is a false and dangerous definition of faith. Now there is evidently an ambiguity in the first part of this proposition. For if it mean that to believe that

Christ intentionally shed his blood for us in particular, and that this is the first thing in order to be believed, then it is indeed a very improper definition of saving faith. But if it mean that Christ as crucified and slain for our salvation, is ours in the offer of the gospel, and by hearty acceptance, consent and appropriation becomes ours in possession, and in this order the believer is warranted to conclude that Christ died intentionally for him; and that he shall assuredly and everlastingly be saved, then it is a true and just definition of faith; and agreeable to the 68th section of the 10th article of our Declaration and Testimony concerning faith, which runs thus: 'We testify all who deny that any persuasion, assurance or confidence, that we in particular, thro' the grace of our Lord Jesus Christ, shall be saved belongs to the nature of saving faith. And also agreeable to the Act concerning the doctrine of Grace, which teaches, that faith consists in believing 'that what Christ did for the redemption of sinners, he did it for us, and that we shall be saved thro' him': The Com. considers it as extremely improper in Mr. Campbell to affirm that the above definition of faith is false and dangerous, without specifying and explaining in what sense he considers it false and dangerous. And by comparing this clause of Mr. C's Reasons of Protest, namely that it is false and dangerous to say that faith includes in it a persuasion or belief, that we in particular shall be saved thro' him, with his declaration wherein he speaks of the assurance of faith, it is evident that whatever he may mean by assurance of faith, he can not mean that it includes in it an assurance that we shall have life and salvation by Christ. Which the Com. thinks a material acknowledgement of the point at issue between P'b'y and Mr. C. For notwithstanding that he speaks of the confidence and assurance of faith, yet it is plain from the tenor of the sentence, and especially from the concluding part of it, that he does not mean to assert that assurance belongs to the nature of faith, but to a high degree of it; for he expressly concludes the sentence thus: 'Wherefore the assurance is not of the essence of faith.' Which words, if they have any direct relation to the point in contest, concerning which he intended to explain himself to P'b'y, clearly mean that assurance does not belong to the lowest degree or very nature of faith; but to a high degree of it. For this and this alone was the precise point in contest between the P'b'y and Mr. C. And the declaration was intended as a correct explanation of Mr. C's mind on that point and that point alone. On this ground it is considerably evident that Mr. C. in his declaration denies the very doctrine which the P'b'y was affirming.

"Mr. C. is charged in the 2nd place with teaching that a church has no divine warrant for confessions of faith, as terms of communion. Comparing what Mr. C. has advanced upon this article in his declarations with what he says in the introduction to his Reasons of Protest, the Com. are of opinion that he has materially acknowledged the charge. The manner in which he speaks in his declarations is evasive and equivocal. Fewer words than he has employed would have given an explicit and satisfactory answer. But instead of saying 'I believe that there is a divine warrant for confessions of faith as terms of communion,' he says 'I believe that the church has all the divine warrant for such exhibitions of the truth, which our Confession and Testimony adduce for that purpose,'—a declaration which he might have made in full consistency with the truth of the charge. And that Mr. C. is opposed to the approbation of Confessions of Faith as a term of admission to the fellowship of the church, there are the strongest grounds to believe from the introduction to his reasons of protest, in which he declares that it was not only his opinion, but that he had taught publicly 'that an agreement in what is expressly taught and enjoined in the New Testament, either in express terms or by an approven precedent, should be deemed sufficient in point of unity and uniformity, and that nothing should be made a term of communion in the Christian Church, which is not as old as the New Testament; or that is not expressly revealed and enjoined therein.'

"On the 3d article, the Com. remarks that if Mr. C. means by ruling elders exhorting publicly in vacant cong'ns, their doing so as what belongs to their office, which indeed appears to be his mind, his encouraging such a practice is inconsistent with preserving the Scripture distinction between the duties of the teaching and ruling elder.

"On the 4th article, which refers to Mr. C's asserting that it is lawful for people of our communion to hear ministers that are in a stated opposition to our Testimony, the Com. remarks that Mr. C. in his declaration plainly teaches that 'it is lawful for them, in the absence of their own minister to hear other ministers when the worship was not corrupted with matters of human invention. And here they may be allowed to add their opinion that it is altogether unwarrantable for a min'r belonging to this Synod to advise his hearers to attend the public administration of those in different communions; the propriety of min'rs doing which however, Mr. C. in his speeches in Synod, has plainly avowed. Upon the whole the Com. are of opinion that Mr. C's answers to the two first articles of charge, especially, are so evasive, unsatisfactory and highly equivocal upon great and important articles of revealed religion as to give ground to conclude that he has expressed sentiments very different upon these articles from the sentiments held and professed by this church; and are sufficient ground to infer censure.' Before agreeing to the concluding paragraph of the report, Mr. C. begged to be heard. He was heard accordingly. The question was then put, Agree to the concluding paragraph or not, and it was agreed to. To this Mr. C. declared his dissent for reasons to be offered in due form. Adjourned to meet at three o'clock." (Closed with prayer.)

3 o'clock p. m. . . .
"Resumed the consideration of Mr. C's cause.

And after some conversation about what censure was due to Mr. C. for what was found against him, a motion was made that Mr. C. be rebuked and admonished, and, if further satisfaction be not received by the Synod, that he be suspended from his office.''

"Minutes of Associate Synod," page 192: "Before taking up this motion it was proposed and agreed to that he should be heard more fully by way of answer to questions or otherwise. Among other questions, the following was put to him, Whether he agreed in sentiment with that passage of the Declaration and Testimony, Art. 13, Sect. 6. 'We testify against all who deny that any persuasion, assurance or confidence, that we in particular, thro' the grace of the Lord Jesus Christ shall be saved, belongs to the nature of faith.' And he answered in the affirmative. In the course of a long conversation, Mr. C. gave such explanations as the Synod considered pretty satisfactory in regard to the 1st, 2d and 3rd articles. On the 4th article, the Synod judged his explanations not satisfactory; and agreed to require that whatever different sentiments he might have on the subject of occasional hearing from the rest of the Synod, he should abstain from teaching them in public or private. He declared his purpose to avoid giving offence on this head as much as possible. On the ground of the above explanations and resolution, the Synod proceeded to consider in what manner the affair should be issued. A motion that it should be by rebuke and admonition. To which an amendment was offered, that it should be by admonition only. After some conversation was put, Rebuke and admonish Mr. Campbell, or admonish only, and it carried. Rebuke and admonish. Mr. C. wished the Synod to delay passing censure, and the Synod delayed until to-morrow. Adjourned to meet at half past 8 o'clock this evening. Closed with prayer.

"Half past 8 o'clock p. m., Synod met, and in the absence of the Mod'r was constituted with prayer by Mr. Laing, last Mod'r. Immediately after prayer, the Mod'r took the chair. Members present as above, together with Mr. Murdoch. Read the minutes of last sitting. A protest with reasons against the deed of Synod reversing the sentence of suspension passed by the P'b'y of Chartiers on Mr. Campbell by Messrs. J. Anderson, Jas. Ramsay, Min'rs, S. Murdock, S. Templeton, Elders, was given in and read. Messrs. Pringle and Shaw were appointed a committee to prepare answers to s'd reasons of protest against next meeting of Synod. Mr. Armstrong wished some instructions to the committee on the petition concerning slavery. Some general conversation ensued, expressive of the unanimous sense the Synod had of the evil of slave-holding. Mr. Campbell gave in a paper called 'A Remonstrance,' stating that he could not submit to censure as proposed because he could not acknowledge the charge found against him, while he was willing to submit to an admonition on the score of imprudence; and requesting the Synod to reconsider their deed concerning him. After some conversation the Synod agreed to reconsider. Adjourned to meet tomorrow morning at 6 o'clock. Closed with prayer."

"Frid., 27, May. Synod met and was opened with prayer by the Mod'r. Members present, except Mr. Campbell and Mr. Murdoch, the latter having leave of absence. A letter from Mr. C. to the Mod'r was received and read, containing grievous charges against the Synod, for their judging him guilty of evasion and equivocation, charges of partiality and injustice, and informing the Synod that he declined their authority. The Synod agreed to summon him to appear immediately to answer for bringing such charges, and for declining their authority. Read the minutes of all the preceding sittings. Mr. C., attending according to summons, was conversed with on the contents of his letter and required to retract the charges against the Synod and submit to their authority. He took back the letter, acknowledging his rashness in bringing such charges and declining the authority of Synod. Adjourned to meet at half past 9 o'clock. Closed with prayer."

"Half past 9 o'clock a. m. Synod met and was open'd with prayer by the Mod'r. Members present as above, except Messrs. Anderson and Laing, Min'rs; Gosman, Murdoch, Templeton and Wallace, Elders, absent on leave. The Synod reconsidered their judgment in the case of Mr. Campbell, finding his answers in the two first articles of charge evasive, unsatisfactory and highly equivocal. A motion was made that the word 'evasive' be erased, and, after some conversation, was agreed to. The question was then put, Adhere to the Synod's deed respecting the censure; namely, Rebuke and admonition or not, and it was carried, Adhere. Mr. C. was then asked if he was ready to submit to censure. After a few remarks he declared his submission. And a brother having been employed in prayer, he was accordingly rebuked and admonished by the Mod'r. And in this manner the affair was issued."

"In the representation made by the members of P'b'y of Chartiers, in regard to the benefit likely to result from the measure, the Synod agreed to divide the s'd P'b'y into two; the one to be called by the present name, the Ass. P'b'y of Chartiers, and to consist of the ministers, together with ruling elders, from the respective sessions of the following Ass. Cong'ns of Cannonsburg, Mt. Hope and Cross Creek, Piny Creek & Monture's Run. And it was appointed that the several Ass. vacancies presently existing or which may hereafter arise to the east of the Ohio, together with the vacancies of Rockbridge, Virg., should belong to s'd P'b'y; the other to be called the Ass. P'b'y of Ohio, and to consist of the min'rs, together with a ruling elder from the respective sessions of the following Ass. Cong'ns." [Here on the page of the minutes was left a blank space for the writing in of the names of the said congregations, but it remains blank to this day.]

On pages 198 and 199 of "Minutes of the Associate Synod" for 1808 there is found the list of appointments, and, last of all, "Mr. Th. Campbell in Phil'a, Jun., July, then in Chartiers till next meeting." So it was thought that the trial for heresy was ended. We have no word as to the activities of Mr. Campbell in Philadelphia during the two months of June and July, 1808.

Chapter V

FAREWELL TO SECEDERISM

AT the Chartiers Meeting-house, on Aug. 2, 1808, the Presbytery met and heard read an extract of the minutes of the Synod which had held its sessions in Philadelphia in May. It is stated on page 178 of Chartiers Presbytery Minutes that Presbytery dissented from Synod's finding that it had been guilty of breach of agreement in its dealing with Mr. Campbell, and also "against removing the suspension from Mr. C. while the grounds of it were not examined." On the following day the members of the Presbytery declared adherence to a testimony that covered the opposite of the first five of the charges against Mr. Campbell.

Chartiers Presbytery had a meeting on Sept. 13, 1808, at Burgettstown. Mr. Campbell, having finished two assigned months of service in the Presbytery of Philadelphia, came to his home Presbytery and found that no assignments had been made for him. On page 183 we find Mr. Campbell asking Presbytery why it had not mapped out a course of service for him. "Reply was not sure that Mr. C. would be within their bounds, as he had signified his intention to be within bounds of Presb'y of Phil'a on account of his family [probably meaning the arrival of his family from Ireland]. Nor had

Mr. C. taken care to inform any of time he would be within our bounds."

"Mr. C. then asked, 'he wished to know on what footing the P'b'y considered him as one of their members.' Presb'y said a member on account of what Synod had done and to be within their bounds."

Then arose a controversy about reports that had been made about him and what purported to be extracts from Synod's minutes. The basis of the controversy possibly was a failure of the clerk of Synod to record all that Mr. Campbell had said when he agreed to submit to censure, for Mr. Campbell repudiated entirely the idea that he had agreed to censure because he had been convinced that he was in error in opinion of doctrine (p. 183). "And to prove these assertions, he proposed to read a paper, which he called an authentic extract of the Synod's procedure in his case, given by Mr. Pringle, the Synod's clerk, and signed by him in the presence of Mr. Armstrong, as this paper (speaking nothing about the report of the Committee upon Mr. Campbel's case and stating that he submitted to censure on condition that his deference to the judgment of brethren and his desire not to appear refractory should be understood as the reason of his submission) appeared so inconsistent with the Extract sent by the Synod's clerk, that the representation given by this paper of the Synod's procedure in Mr. Campbel's case might be justly deemed partial and even false; the Presb'y therefore agreed to read the official extract. Which being done, Mr. Campbel declared that this extract was a very unfair and unjust account of what was done in Synod, as it contained a report of the Committee upon his case which was different from their true report to the Synod, and which he never heard read in Synod, and as it did not contain the condition mentioned in his paper upon which he said he had submitted to censure."

Thus reads the report of the Committee which is referred to, but it would seem that it had not stuck in the minds of the delegates from Chartiers to the Synod that after the report of the Committee which found Mr. Campbell guilty, and that his "answers to the first two articles of charge especially are so evasive, unsatisfactory and highly equivocal . . . and are sufficient ground to infer censure," it was allowed that Mr. Campbell should be heard more fully (pp. 192, 193 and 194). The Synod's clerk wrote in the minutes, "In the course of a long conversation, Mr. C. gave such explanations as the Synod considered pretty satisfactory in regard to the 1st, 2d and 3rd articles. On the 4th article the Synod judged his explanations not satisfactory; and agreed to require that whatever sentiments he might have on the subject of occasional hearing from the rest of the Synod, he should abstain from teaching them in public or private. He declared his purpose to avoid giving offense on this head as much as possible. On the ground of the above explanations and resolution the Synod proceeded to consider in what manner the affair should be issued." It will be seen, therefore, that after seeming to accept the report of the Committee, Synod heard Mr. Campbell and was persuaded that he was less a heretic than the report of the Committee made him out to be. Its action and minutes virtually reverse the report of the Committee, and this fact was not weighed, it seems, by the Presbytery of Chartiers. It must be recalled also that Mr. Campbell resented the words "evasive, unsatisfactory and highly equivocal" in the report of the committee, and gave notice of reasons of dissent that he proposed to present. Mr. Campbell handed in a "remonstrance" on the afternoon of May 26, and through it gained the consent of Synod to reconsider their deed concerning him (p. 195). At a meeting at 6:00 o'clock in the morning of May 27, Mr. Campbell was represented by a letter that bore heavily against Synod for adjudging him guilty of evasion and equivocation, charged Synod with partiality and injustice, and declined their authority (p. 196). He was summoned in person after the letter had been read and agreed to take back his letter. At the 9:30 o'clock meeting, morning of May 27, as we read on page 197, "The Synod reconsidered their judgment in the case of Mr. Campbell, finding his answers on the two first articles of charge evasive, unsatisfactory and highly equivocal. A motion was made that the word 'evasive' be erased, and after some conversation was agreed to."

Richardson's *Memoirs of Alexander Campbell* (Vol. I., p. 229) deals with this phase of the trial.

He reports the findings of the Committee on the first two articles of charge, but fails to notice what has been stressed here; namely, that Mr. Campbell had virtually cleared himself, before Synod, of fault as to the first three articles of libel, and that he had secured the elimination from the report of the committee of the obnoxious word "evasive," though one wonders why he did not object just as strenuously to "highly equivocal." It can be seen that if the Presbytery of Chartiers was basing its report and state of the case upon the report of the Synod committee only, it was thoroughly misrepresenting the action and stand of Synod and also the attitude of Mr. Campbell. Moreover, if the clerk of Synod had furnished as extracts just the report of the committee and not the actions that followed as pointed out above, and if Mr. Campbell, because he was the most interested person, had included in his papers such items as have been set forth and documented, it could be seen how that Presbytery might be thinking in terms of additions to the minutes of Synod on Mr. Campbell's part, and he of suppressions on the part of the Presbytery.

Passing again to the session of Presbytery at Burgettstown on Sept. 13, 1808 ("Minutes Chartiers Presbytery," p. 184), we read between the lines that there must have been rather sharp words and possibly charges of falsehood, with the result that Mr. Campbell took from the hands of the clerk of Presbytery the paper that he had presented as a copy of the minutes of Synod concerning his case, and "then in his own name and in the name of all who adhered to him, he declined the authority of this Presbytery for reasons formerly given, the authority of the Associate Synod of North America and all the courts subordinate thereto; and all further communion with them. He then offered to read another paper, which he said, contained reasons for his declinature. He was directed to lay this paper on the Presbytery's table; but he refused to do so. And having been told that unless he did so, it would be improper to permit the reading of it; and being further interrogated about it, it was a letter he had given in to the Synod at their last meeting, declining their authority: acknowledging that he had then taken it back, but since that time had seen cause to adhere to it." The lateness of the hour brought on an adjournment.

On the succeeding day, September 14, Mr. Campbell was not present, but there was noted a letter from him which was a "Declinature the same as the previous verbal one." This paper is probably the one which is given in full on pages 17 and 18 of *Memoirs of Elder Thomas Campbell,* of which so much was thought that he had diligently preserved it, although the paper bears no date nor address. In the same Mr. Campbell makes reference to Mr. Ramsey especially as diligently demanding before the Synod the issue of a trial. It was the unanimous opinion that Mr. Campbell's conduct demanded censure. Action was taken that he immediately be suspended from ministerial office, "which sentence was accordingly pronounced by the Moderator as the mouth of the Presbytery in the name of the Lord Jesus." The reasons of suspension proceeded upon are based unjustly, it seems to the writer, upon the report of the committee, which was modified by the Synod, and really and in fact destroyed, as shown above. However, here follow the reasons for the suspension of Mr. Campbell: 1. "That Mr. C. denies that he has any conviction of having expressed erroneous sentiments as has been specified by the Committee of the Synod upon his case, and also denies that he submitted to censure on any such account, thus he places himself in precisely the same situation he was in when the Synod judged him worthy of censure, and agreed that if satisfaction were not given by him, he should be suspended from his office: he forfeits all the privilege he was to have obtained by submitting to censure and makes it necessary for the Presb'y to carry the Synod's resolution into effect, and he must necessarily be considered as still under process. 2. That by declining the authority of the Ass. Synod and of this Presb'y and of all other courts belonging to the Synod, he tramples upon all authority which alone gave him any right to exercise the office of a minister. 3. That he declines the authority of the Synod and Presb'y and their communion without so much as presuming to find fault with the doctrine, worship and government maintained by these courts. 4. That the instances of discipline he pretends to complain of in the procedure of the Presb'y and Synod, were no other than what he had submitted before to the Synod at

Philadelphia before he came into the bounds of this Presbytery and take his seat in it by appointment of Synod; and therefore they cannot be the grounds of his declining their authority now...."
"Mr. Campbell was appointed to be cited to attend at their next meeting in order to be further dealt with. It was agreed that intimation should be made of the suspension of Mr. Campbel to all the congregations belonging to this Presbytery and to the other Presby's belonging to the Synod."

In minutes of a sitting of Presbytery at Monture's Run Meetinghouse on Nov. 2, 1808, we read: "The clerk was appointed to send citation to the Rev'd Thomas Campbell . . . to appear in the next Presb'y meeting to be farther dealt with." Nothing is read about Mr. Campbell's case until on May 3 at Mt. Pleasant Meetinghouse in the following year of 1809. Then it is "A draught of Remonstrance against certain decisions and steps of procedure of the Associate Synod in the case of Mr. Campbel having been produced by the Com. appointed to prepare was read and ordered sent to the Synod. Transcript also of procedure in Mr. C's case since last meeting of the Synod."

So again we go to the session of Synod, this time at Philadelphia. It began that year of 1809 on May 17, but not until the third day, May 19, do we find the case taken up. On page 202 of "Minutes of Associate Synod," we read: "Read an extract from the minutes of the P'b'y of Chartiers, stating that in Sept. last Mr. Th. Campbell had declined s'd p'b'y, this Synod and all courts subordinate thereto, and that they had suspended him from his office; and requesting the Synod's advice as to further procedure in his case. Appointed Messrs. Pringle, Smith, Hamilton and Bruce a committee to consider and report on the advice to be given to the p'b'y of Chartiers on the case referred to. On motion, Resolved that considering it appears from the minutes of the p'b'y of Chartiers that Mr. Campbell has declined as aforesaid his name should be erased from the roll. Mr. Campbell gave in a paper entitled 'Declaration and Address to the Ass. Synod; and s'd paper was referred to the committee now appointed.'" In the afternoon of May 19, report was called for from the committee to whom had been committed Mr. Campbell's last paper, and it was this: "That Mr. Campbell have liberty to withdraw his paper, because it recognizes his declinature of subjection to this Synod, reflects on the p'b'y of Chartiers in his own case, and contains proposals inconsistent with our received principles." Before a vote was taken the paper itself was read. We know nothing of the contents except from the few words in the committee's report, but the report was agreed to. Then "Mr. Campbell craved extracts and it was agreed to." On page 203 is found the report of the committee that was to draught advice for the Presbytery of Chartiers, and it was this: "That the p'b'y either sist further process or proceed according to ordinary rules, to inflict higher censure, as the nature of the case may require, or the state of the church render necessary and expedient." Then the minutes of the Synod are taken up with the matters at issue between them and the Presbytery of Chartiers. The Presbytery was determined to secure a rescinding of Synod's stand as to their first judgment against Mr. Campbell. The Rev's John Anderson and James Ramsay were the Presbytery's representatives, and they remonstrated up to such point that finally, on May 20, the Synod dismissed their protests on several grounds, the first which reads: "Because of the indecency of the language, charging the Synod with arrogance, weakness, folly, &c., besides other harsh expressions unfit to be used in any case, especially by an inferior court to a superior" (p. 209). On Tuesday, May 23, 1809, occurs the notation: "A letter inclosing a Fifty Dollar note, refunding a like sum given him by the Synod in May, 1807, was rec'd from Mr. Th. Campbell. The clerk was directed to give him a receipt." On Wednesday, May 24, a synodical letter was adopted, and the same was spread on the minutes. On page 217 there is a paragraph which may be interpreted as relating to Mr. Campbell as well as to others: "We have heard with concern of the separation from you of some brethren with whom you took sweet counsel and walked together to the house of God. By this distressing occurrence parties are multiplied, animosity excited, temptations to unsteadfastness in profession extended, and occasions given to the enemies of the Lord to triumph. Tho such a division must cause great searching and grief of heart, we rejoice in beholding your order and steadfastness in the faith and patience in the kingdom of our Lord Jesus Christ."

"p. s. It is thought necessary to inform you that Mr. John Smith was deposed for scandal in 1806. And Mr. Peter McMillan for D'r [short for 'drunkenness'] in 1807. And that Mr. Th. Campbell has declined the authority of the Synod and is suspended." Thus they classed Mr. Campbell with scandal-mongers and drunkards, but said nothing of those ministers of Chartiers Presbytery who were resolved to undo Mr. Campbell by impoverishing him, by misrepresenting his state with Synod and provoking him to take the step which gave the reverend brethren of the Presbytery excuse to unfrock him.

Chartiers Presbytery was not yet done with Mr. Campbell, even though he had repaid his monetary obligation to the Synod. At Chartiers Meeting-house on July 4, 1809, this action was taken: "On motion the question was put Sist procedure in Mr. Campbel's case or proceed according to the rules of the church. Carried to proceed. A summons ordering Mr. C. to appear at next meeting of Presb'y."

"Burgettstown, Aug. 5, 1809. . . . Received information that Mr. C. had been served with a summons to appear at this meeting according to the appointment of last meeting, but on being called, he was found to be not present. Wherefore appointed to be served with another summons at the next ordinary meeting at Chartiers on the

FAREWELL TO SECEDERISM 97

last Wed. of October." But in the record of that meeting on Oct. 26, 1809, there is no note of the name of Mr. Campbell or action that touched him. And not until on April 17 of the following year, 1810, do we come to the real end of the matter on Presbytery's part. At the meeting at Mt. Pleasant Meeting-house, Mr. Alison reported that the third citation had been delivered to Mr. Campbell. Then there is noted "A paper subscribed by Mr. Campbel in answer to the citations that had been sent him by the Presb'y." Nothing appears to indicate the nature of that paper, whether hostile, concilatory, appealing, or what. On the following day, April 18, we discover the following as a part of the minutes of Presbytery's actions: "The Presb'y having agreed to enter upon the consideration of Mr. Campbel's case, the minutes of Presb'y respecting his suspension were read and also his answer sent in writing to Presby's last citation. After considering this answer, and finding that it contained nothing to stop procedure in his case, the question was put, 'Inflict higher censure upon Mr. C. for the reasons of his suspension specified in the minutes of the Presby's meeting at Burgettstown, on Sept. 14, 1808, and for contumacy in not appearing to answer the citations that have been sent him, or not?' Question carried in the affirmative. After which, and a member having been employed in prayer, the question was first put, Whether or not the censure that ought to be inflicted in this case be deposition and suspension from sealing ordinances?

Which was carried in the affirmative. After which another question—to be inflicted now? Carried in the affirmative. Accordingly the Presbytery did and hereby do depose Mr. Campbel from the office of the Holy Ministry, and from sealing ordinances for the reasons above mentioned. Agreed to send an extract of this deposition of Mr. Campbell to the Synod and to intimate it to the congregations under our inspection.''

So ends on page 206 of the "Minutes of Chartiers Presbytery" the relation of Mr. Thomas Campbell with the same Presbytery in their estimation. But it had been much earlier in the mind of Mr. Campbell, for he had been studying the matters of church authority, creeds and confessions of faith, and the divisions that were extant among the people of God.

Rather early in 1809, Mr. Campbell had conceived the idea of forming a Christian Association, which should not be a church, but an agency for helping to propagate the ideas of Christian union. He had found many sympathetic hearers, and they were described as "persons of different religious denominations, most of them in an unsettled state as to a fixed gospel ministry." At a formal meeting at Buffalo, Aug. 17, 1809, twenty-one of those present were named to meet and confer together, and with the assistance of Elder Thomas Campbell to determine upon the proper means to carry into effect the important ends of their Association (The Christian Association of Washington). Out of that appointment and the conferences which followed came the "Declaration and Address," which has created a profound impression ever since its publication.

It is very unfair and unjust that there should appear in the biographical sketch of Thomas Campbell in the *Manual of the United Presbyterian Church,* which church has fallen heir to some of the Seceder congregations and ministers referred to in this account, a statement that the body, which grew up out of the foundations which Thomas Campbell was discovering in the last years of his life as a Seceder minister, has both a written and an unwritten creed. From the days when their most bitter and insulting enemies called them derisively "Campbellites" or "Campbellite Baptists," through the period when the name "Reformers" and "Restorers" had some vogue, until these present days, in which they have in brotherly fashion been conceded the right to call themselves and be called "Christians," "Disciples of Christ" and their congregations "Churches of Christ" or "Christian Churches" (but none of these names exclusively), there is not to be found an individual or a congregational group, claiming or acknowledging a written (in the sense of humanly composed) or an unwritten creed. Mr. Campbell never felt that he was making one in the "Declaration and Address," never encouraged any one so to think of it, nor did he ever urge any one over whom he had influence to prepare and publish a creed to take the place of any already in the field of religion. He grew out of the creeds to which the Seceder body gave allegiance and came to feel that nothing ought to take the place of the Bible, especially the New Testament, in the life and attention of a church or an individual.

Chapter VI

ONE SHIP ARRIVES

IN 1808 Thomas Campbell's loving wife and seven children (three sons and four daughters) were still across the Atlantic Ocean in Ireland. That wife, if she had been in America, would have been a great source of comfort and aid to Mr. Campbell through the two and more stormy years that have been described. Even the oldest son, Alexander, who had been bearing up nobly as teacher in the seminary over which his father had installed him when he left for America, and as the head of the family, would have been able to temper the sorrow of his father while resting under the disapproval of his fellow ministers. Of course, there were exchanges of letters, but the eighty or ninety days required for the same, left long weeks of anxiety and uncertainty. In spite of his being more or less an object of dislike and suspicion on the part of the ministers in Chartiers Presbytery, Mr. Campbell never thought of returning to Ireland. He was even more determined to have his family join him in Washington, Pa., where he had established his headquarters. He had evidently expected that his loved ones might arrive in July or August of 1808, for that would seem to explain the two months' appointment which had been given to him in the Presbytery of Philadelphia—

June and July of 1808. But smallpox had broken out at Rich Hill. Some of the younger children of the Campbell family had become infected. Jane, the fourth child, suffered a very severe attack, and was left sorely disfigured. The other children had the disease in much milder form. Preparations for the journey to America thus interrupted, were resumed in August. Alexander went to Londonderry and booked passage for his mother, sisters and brothers on the ship "Hibernia." It seemed to be an unlucky vessel. It was slow in getting ready to sail; was undermanned; had a captain who was stubborn and bibulous; and some of the crew were young and inexperienced. The ship made a false start on September 28, and another on October 1. On October 2 it got into the Atlantic, but a stop was made for the sake of securing a supply of whisky not far from Innishowen. The next day saw another effort to get away, but a high and adverse wind drove the vessel all night, and morning found it along the coast of Scotland near the island of Islay. The captain elected to stay in the rather dangerous place even though there was a better harbor near by. Near midnight of October 7, because of a severe gale, the ship dragged her anchors and hit on a sunken rock. Richardson [*Memoirs,* Vol. I., p. 100] relates that earlier in the evening while dozing, Alexander had a very vivid dream which anticipated the shipwreck. As a result, he remained dressed except for his shoes, and was ready for the emergency which arose. For the full description of the wreck and the rescue, we refer the reader to the work above cited.

Only God knows what would have been the course of Alexander Campbell's life if the shipwreck had not occurred, or what would have been the results on Thomas Campbell's life if his brilliantly endowed son and the family had arrived in America in 1808 as had been planned. After he had given such aid as he could to all in rescuing life and property, the son on the deck of the wrecked vessel gave himself to meditation, and it issued in his giving himself to the same great work in which his father was engaged—the ministry of the gospel. The family lost rather severely in goods, but ever after felt that the wreck turned out to their advantage. It seemed best to all that they should go to Glasgow, and they lodged themselves in that great city of learning, where from Nov. 8, 1808, until the close of the session in May of 1809, Alexander was a student in the university. He did not need the presence of a father to prod him on. He allowed himself but six hours of sleep at night. French, New Testament Greek, Classical Greek, Latin, Logic, Belles Lettres, Experimental Philosophy were his studies. Two of his professors had been over his father more than twenty-five years before. By way of diversion, Alexander read very widely, attended special lectures and conversations, and heard the preaching of some of the great religious leaders of the day. He was not afraid to hear them, for his independence of mind held him back from counting any one of them as his master in religion. The two brothers Haldane seemed to influence him more than others. The splendid liberality of the older Haldane moved the young man to adopt financial independence as a plan, with the result that Alexander Campbell was a liberal man and preached the gospel without fee or reward as long as he lived. At the close of the university year, it was impossible to turn their faces again toward America. So the young student was persuaded to engage in some tutoring for a couple of months on the north shore of the Clyde.

On Aug. 5, 1809, we discover the Campbell family embarking to join the father in the New World. The ship soon sprung a leak, but the captain would not turn back. The crew and passengers nursed their craft along, but it was a stormy voyage. A high wind carried away a mast and its sail, and a later dreadful storm shredded the remaining sails. A passing vessel, westward bound, kindly furnished the almost bestilled ship with a sail. Good and bad weather continued and struggled for the mastery of the vessel, but finally, on September 29, the anchor was dropped in New York harbor. A few days were spent in the city of New York. On October 7 the family that had been so delayed by disease and an unfriendly ocean arrived in Philadelphia. Within two days they were on the last lap of their journey in a conestoga wagon. Westward three hundred and fifty miles over the plains and mountains of Pennsylvania were the loving husband and father and the new home they had been longing for. The way by which the heavenly Father had been leading them was hard and stormy and devious, but it came to a peaceful and happy end.

Chapter VII

EXAMINATION OF AN "ADDRESS"

IN the year and several months of this interim, Thomas Campbell had not been idle. He had made a clean break with the Presbyterians. In a previous chapter, the minutes of Chartiers Presbytery have been cited to show that on Sept. 13, 1808, he renounced the authority of both the lower and higher court of the Associate Churches. That lower court retorted by suspending him, on September 14, from all ministerial functions. It therefore seems proper to use the date, September 13, as that which marked Mr. Campbell's actual separation from Secederism.

"In bidding adieu to Secederism, he made on that occasion, the following address:*

"Taking into my most serious consideration, the present state of matters between this reverend Synod and myself, upon a review of the whole process and issue as commenced and conducted, first by the Presbytery of Chartiers, and as now issued by this reverend court, I can not help thinking myself greatly aggrieved. For, although this Synod in part redressed the grievance I labored under by the hasty, unprecedented, and unjustifiable proceedings of said Presbytery, in holding

---
*A. Campbell, *Memoirs of Elder Thomas Campbell,''* pp. 17, 18.

me to the issue of a trial contrary to their manifest agreement, under the preliminary that no witnesses should be cited on either side, yet, in the issue, that Presbytery is dismissed from the bar of this Synod without the slightest notice of the sin and scandal of this breach of faith, and avowed dissimulation; for Mr. Ramsey declared, at the bar of this Synod, that it was the intention of the Presbytery to hold me to the issue of the trial, at all events. And also, without any inquiry into the *other* grounds and reasons (though professedly wishing for an accommodation by explications) of my avowed declinature of any further ministerial connection with, or subjection to, that Presbytery in its present corrupt state (as specified in my reasons of protest and declinature given into this Synod), yet this Synod, after examining my written declarations to said Presbytery upon the articles of libel, and after a long and close examination of my principles relative to said articles; and not being able to point out a single error in the former, and declaring themselves satisfied with the latter (the article upon occasional hearing excepted), yet proceeded to find me guilty of evasion and equivocation, in my written declarations, upon great and important articles of revealed religion; and thence infer that I had expressed sentiments upon these articles very different from sentiments held and professed by this Church, and upon these presumptions proceed to judge me worthy of a solemn rebuke; while as I have observed above, no notice is taken of the Presbytery's breach of faith and avowed dissimulation and flagrant injustice toward me, while acting as a court of Jesus Christ, nor of any act of their mal-administration toward others, which I alleged against them, and referred to, as just grounds for my said declinature, as contained in my reasons of protest, and in other documents read and laid upon the table for the inspection of the Synod. Surely, if presumptive evasion and equivocation justly infer a censure of rebuke on my part, their manifest breach of faith and avowed dissimulation (I might add *treachery*), can not be innocent and unrebukable conduct. Of the justness and propriety of this, let the world judge.

"It is with sincere reluctance, and, at the same time, with all due respect and esteem for the brethren of this reverend Synod who have presided in the trial of my case, that I find myself in duty bound to refuse submission to their decision as *unjust* and *partial;* and *finally to decline their* authority, while they continue thus to overlook the grievous and *flagrant mal-administration of the Presbytery of Chartiers.* And I hereby do decline all ministerial connection with, or subjection to, the Associate Synod of North America, on account of the aforesaid corruptions and grievances; and do henceforth hold myself altogether unaffected by their decisions. And that I may be properly understood, I will distinctly state that while especial reference is had to the corruptions of *the Presbytery* of Chartiers, which constitute only a part of this Synod, *the corruptions of that Pres-*

bytery now become also the corruptions of the whole Synod; because when laid open to this Synod, and unprotested against, the Synod pass them over without due inquiry and without animadversion.

"THOMAS CAMPBELL."

The writer is almost, if not quite, persuaded that the above document was not the final one which its writer presented. If one reads carefully the events and record of the trial as it is found in Chapter IV., and then turns to the above letter, it seems that he will conclude that this is the letter which Thomas Campbell sent to the Synod when it met at six o'clock in the morning of Friday, May 27, which letter he withdrew after the Synod had summoned him into its presence. It will be seen that Mr. Ramsey is the particular brother who is mentioned in the above letter, and the chapter referred to shows the activities of Mr. Ramsey against Mr. Campbell. Moreover, the letter above contains the obnoxious phrase "guilty of evasion and equivocation." As was pointed out before, the findings of the committee were amended so as to strike out the word "evasive," leaving only "unsatisfactory and highly equivocal" against him. Would he not have been too careful to have included the word "evasion" in his farewell address, knowing that it had not been left as a part of the report of the committee to investigate his case? The letter that has been spread in detail in this chapter seems to have done another duty. In Chapter V., Mr. Campbell hands in a written "declinature," and when interrogated about it, informs the Presbytery that it was the same that he had handed in at the meeting of the last Synod, had withdrawn and now had seen reason for holding to its contentions. As additional evidence, that the letter which Alexander Campbell considered as his father's last message to the Associate Synod was not the last, but must have been another that has been entirely lost, we ask that the reader turn again to Chapter V and read of the actions of the Synod in the year 1809. Mr. Campbell gave in a paper entitled "Declaration and Address to the Ass. Synod," and the same was referred to a committee. On May 19 the report of that committee was made. The last part of the report runs, "and contains proposals inconsistent with our received principles." Now the "adieu letter" under consideration lacks entirely any proposals that have to do with the received principles of Secederism. It is denunciatory of both presbytery and Synod, involves both in the same guilt and dismisses the writer from further fellowship and association with them. It contains no proposals for anything. How we long for some of those remonstrances and letters that Thomas Campbell sent to the table from time to time!* They would help to throw more light on the trial and its sequel.

---

*It is reported that several decades ago, two young men, connected with the Campbell family fed a bonfire with letters, essays, pamphlets and such things that they had found in the old Campbell homestead at Bethany, W. Va.—possibly some of the very things which historical students would love to peruse and use as they write about the elder and younger Campbell. If the report is true, "the aspiring youth that fired the Ephesian dome" has modern rivals.

When we recall that the last letter which Mr. Campbell handed to Synod bore the title "Declaration and Address," and remember that it was the year 1809, and the month of May, is it hard to believe that something of the great and well-known "Declaration and Address" had been passed in for the Synod's attention; that there were contained some of the proposals with which we have become familiar? Of course, not in the complete style that was wrought out after months of thinking and preaching upon the subjects involved.

Chapter VIII

A NEW TITLE AND A GREAT MOTTO

SOME great men of biblical lore gained for themselves a new or additional name. Abram became Abraham; Jacob was turned into Israel; Simon, son of Jonas, was surnamed Peter by his Lord. It seems just as fitting to bestow a new name or title upon Thomas Campbell at this juncture. For about thirty years he had been under the name "Seceder." Together with that we would include that he was a Christian. He has divested himself of that sectarian distinguishing title. He remains a Christian, but because of his particular belief and activity, we could well bestow upon him the title, "advocate of Christian union." He had since the beginning of his Christian life joined with the Thomas of the apostolic circle in saying of Jesus of Nazareth, "My Lord and my God." This new title is not suggested because it is felt that Thomas Campbell was adding something to universal Christian belief and activity. This new emphasis was made necessary because it was an integral part of the Christian faith that had been neglected, obscured, forgotten or even by some unknown.

Mr. Campbell's effort that had been made in Ireland to unite Burgher and anti-Burgher has already been noticed. The Synod in Glasgow had

A New Title and a Great Motto 113

overridden the desire of the presbyteries and the subsidiary Synod in Erin's isle. In that we discover Thomas Campbell as an advocate of Church union or reunion. The charges upon which the heresy trial were based and Mr. Campbell's attitude indicated his interest in a closer fellowship with other sorts of Presbyterians, for he did not "fence the table" in the usual manner. By way of parenthesis—it is never brought out in the testimony of any of the witnesses what or how many aliens from the commonwealth of the anti-Burghers availed themselves of the unfenced table there in Conemaugh. Through his practice and encouragement of "occasional hearing," Mr. Campbell was paving the way for a friendly fellowship if not an eccleciastical relationship, with almost any worthy Christian teacher. But he was too far in advance of the standards of his church and of the ministry that ousted him. He was led of the Word of God to go beyond church union, sectarian toleration and occasional Christian fellowship. The passing of the era of denominationalism and sectarianism, of the rule and domination of creeds, of intolerance of opinions on things not clearly revealed, and the ushering in of the one church of Christ and its corresponding names, of the Bible only and of Christian love and toleration were in the future to engage the thought and labors of Thomas Campbell. The two experiences with Synods and the one with a presbytery were sufficient to give Mr. Campbell a bias against ecclesiastical organizations. But his study of the Bible was also inclining him toward independency and congregationalism.

A smaller man might have yielded to an impulse to divide the churches where he had been ministering and had established contacts. A spur to such action might have been the continued effort of Chartiers Presbytery to have Mr. Campbell appear before it, acknowledge its authority and his heresy. Spies were sent to the meetings that he began to hold and a check was kept upon his movements. The action of Presbytery on Apr. 18, 1810, in deposing the minister who had already renounced their authority, was of a piece with the digging up of the remains of the great Wycliffe that they might be burned. The victim of Secederism was dead to it, and had been for almost a year to its authority and fellowship. However, the church authorities saw some virtue, aside from fulfilling ecclesiastical law, in formally defrocking their former fellow minister and leaving him naked of clerical rights. The "Minutes of the Associate Synod" for 1808 noted that in addition to Mr. Campbell's appeal and protest there had been received "Petitions from Buffaloe, Chartiers, Mt. Pleasant and Burgettstown in favor of Mr. Campbell." Neither Alexander Campbell nor Robert Richardson makes mention of those petitions, if they knew of their existence; nor is there record that the same were acted upon in any way by the Synod. The total number of the petitioners, as well as the number from each place is a profound secret. But the sympathizers with Mr. Campbell seemed to remain constant, for when their friend renounced all claims of the Presbytery upon him, he did so "in the name of all who adhered to him." It is here suggested that the reverend members of Chartiers Presbytery in following Mr. Campbell to the extreme of their ability to hinder him from functioning as a minister and "sealing ordinances" might have had a hope that his friends would be alienated from him, stripped as he was from all ministerial honor and power. If so, they mistook their people. Never for an instant did it seem to cross the deposed minister's mind that he should cease from teaching and preaching. His call had been from on high, and as long as his conscience was clear before the Head of the church, associations of men could not cancel that call.

There is no indication that Mr. Campbell, deprived of the right to be called "Reverend," was less acceptable to the many who had come to look upon him as aggrieved, persecuted and unjustly condemned. They saw in him the same spiritual, talented, biblical, trustworthy and zealous Christian and preacher as before. They opened their houses, barns, yards and groves for his services. The last paid service of Mr. Campbell as a Seceder must have been for those two months in which he labored in the Philadelphia Presbytery. From that time we are able to discover but little about his financial condition. His hearers must have counted him as a laborer worthy of his hire. Out of the considerable number of those who attended his services, there began to emerge a more regular and constant group. Although not many took any formal step of separation from their church, they saw in Mr. Campbell a preacher who fed their souls and a free man who owed no allegiance to any earthly group. The sacred Scriptures were the touchstone of his loyalty. His heart began to be filled with a yearning that Christians everywhere might be one.

The piety and intelligence of Mr. Campbell's hearers naturally led them into the same dissatisfaction with existing religious parties, their intolerant and sectarian spirit which Mr. Campbell felt. They began to give more heed to the Bible as a rule of faith and life. We are not sure as to the party relationship of all those first adherents of the Christian Association. But at the first informal meetings the hearings were large. After several weeks (or months) of meetings, Mr. Campbell "proposed a special meeting, in order to elicit a clear and distinct statement of the principles they advocated" (Richardson's *Memoirs,* Vol. I, p. 235). This was agreed to and a very large concourse of people heard Thomas Campbell at that meeting talk of the evils of division, the sufficiency of the Scriptures, the folly of extraneous theories and opinions, and urge upon all a return to the Scriptures. As a final word he announced a rule by which they had been acting, and he trusted they would act to the end. That rule was "Where the Scriptures speak, we speak; and where the Scriptures are silent, we are silent." Richardson, who knew both the Campbells, states that "from the moment these sig-

A NEW TITLE AND A GREAT MOTTO 117

nificant words were uttered and accepted, the more intelligent ever afterward dated *the formal and actual commencement of the Reformation* which was subsequently carried on with so much success, and which has already produced such important changes in religious society over a large portion of the world" (Richardson's *Memoirs,* Vol. I, p. 237). After some moments of profound thought upon the "Rule," people began to express themselves. The rule was at first like a bombshell to explode and scatter. Infant baptism was seen by some as an institution that would have to be surrendered. After that meeting many ceased to meet with the group, counting some things that they had been holding in their religious lives as too dear to be sacrificed to the rule that Mr. Campbell had announced. Some of the adherents, and even outsiders, began to confront him with his rule and endeavor to show how he was inconsistent. But a considerable number were left, not united in everything, but interested in trying to bring union and peace in the ranks of Christians.

Chapter IX

CHRISTIAN ASSOCIATION—ITS DECLARATION

AUG. 17, 1809, was the date of the formal constitution of the Christian Association of Washington. "Twenty-one of their number were appointed to meet and confer together, and with the assistance of Thomas Campbell, minister of the gospel, to determine upon the proper means to carry into effect the important ends of their Association; the result of which conference was the (following) 'Declaration and Address,' agreed upon and ordered to be printed, at the expense and for the benefit of the society, Sept. 7, 1809" (A. Campbell, *Memoirs of Elder Thomas Campbell*, p. 25). How much the specified number aided in the construction of the great document, we are not informed. It went forth with the name of Thomas Acheson joined to that of Thomas Campbell. But while Thomas Campbell was thinking and writing, probably all of them were helping to construct a meeting-house near to the abiding-place of the "Advocate of Christian Union." The Mr. Acheson mentioned above was a general, and possibly it was thought that his name would carry some weight. And it had been noised abroad that upon hearing that Mr. Campbell's "rule" would terminate infant baptism as a church ordinance, Mr. Acheson had left the place of meeting weeping copious tears over what seemed to be the renunciation of the Saviour's words, "Suffer the little children to come unto me" (Richardson's *Memoirs*, Vol. I., p. 238). His name on the new "Declaration and Address" would indicate that he had come to another understanding of the Saviour's words.

The document of the Christian Association is a rather long treatise, consisting of almost thirty-five 16mo pages, and an Appendix of almost fifty pages. The *Declaration* relates particularly to the purposes, methods of procedure and organization of the Christian Association of Washington. Under nine paragraphs are elucidated the name, monetary support for a pure gospel ministry and supplying the poor with the Holy Scriptures, organizing similar associations, disavowal of the Society's being a church, countenancing and supporting such ministers as conform to the original standard in conversation and doctrine, a standing committee of twenty-one, semi-annual meetings of the society, a program of semi-annual meetings and an avowal of duty to support the ministers engaged by the society. The *Address* embraces a section in which the evils of division are detailed in tender fashion, the need of preaching and worship in sparsely settled areas, the duties of Christians to remedy the pitiable situation and the timeliness and righteousness of the proposals of the Washington Association. The heart of the *Address* is found in thirteen propositions, which are not to be viewed as a new standard or term of communion, but rather "designed for opening up the way that we may come fairly to original ground upon clear and certain premises, and take up things just as the apostles left them; that thus disentangled from the accruing embarrassments of intervening ages, we may stand with evidence upon the same ground on which the church stood at the beginning" (*Memoirs of Elder Thomas Campbell*, p. 48).

Feeling that the propositions in full may be too long, we insert a leading sentence or two from each one.

Proposition 1. The church of Christ on earth is essentially, intentionally and constitutionally one; consisting of all those in every place that profess their faith in Christ and obedience to Him in all things according to the Scriptures. . . .

Proposition 2. Though the church of Christ upon earth must exist in particular and distinct societies, locally separate one from another, yet there ought to be no schisms, no uncharitable divisions among them. . . .

Proposition 3. Nothing ought to be inculcated upon Christians as articles of faith, nor required of them as terms of communion, but what is expressly taught and enjoined upon them in the Word of God. Nor ought anything to be admitted, as of divine obligation, in their church constitution and management, but what is expressly enjoined by the authority of our Lord Jesus Christ and His apostles upon the New Testament church, either in express terms or by approved precedent. . . .

Proposition 4. Although Old and New Testaments are inseparably connected . . . yet the

New Testament is as perfect a constitution for the worship, discipline and government of the New Testament church as the Old Testament was for the Old Testament church. . . .

Proposition 5. The commands and ordinances of our Lord Jesus Christ are to be observed so as to answer the obvious ends of their institution. Human authority has no power to impose new commands or ordinances upon the church, which our Lord Jesus Christ has not enjoined. Nothing ought to be received into the faith and worship of the church or be made a term of communion among Christians, that is not as old as the New Testament. . . .

Proposition 6. Deductions and inferential truths ought to have no place in the church's confession. . . .

Proposition 7. Doctrinal exhibitions of the great system of divine truths and defensive testimonies in opposition to prevailing errors . . . ought not to be made terms of communion. . . .

Proposition 8. It is not necessary that persons should know and apprehend all divinely revealed truths in order to entitle them to a place in the church. Knowledge of self as lost, of the way of salvation through Christ, accompanied with a profession of their faith in, and obedience to, Him . . . is all that is absolutely necessary for admission into His church.

Proposition 9. There should be mutual love and fellowship.

Proposition 10. Division among the Christians is a horrid evil fraught with many evils. It is anti-Christian, anti-scriptural, anti-natural. . . .

Proposition 11. Partial neglect of the expressly revealed will of God, and an assumed authority that puts human opinions and human inventions as a term of communion, introducing them into the constitution, faith or worship of the church, are causes of division and corruption in the church.

Proposition 12. Deals with conditions of membership, continuance in fellowship, ministers teaching the Word of God, and keeping close to the observance of all divine ordinances, after the example of the primitive church exhibited in the New Testament; without any addition whatsoever of human opinions or inventions of men.

Proposition 13. If any circumstantials indispensably necessary to the observance of divine ordinances be not found upon the page of express revelation, such and such only as are absolutely necessary should be adopted under the title of *human expedients.* . . .

This very fine summary deserves attention: "To prepare the way for a permanent scriptural unity among Christians, by calling up to their consideration fundamental truths, directing their attention to first principles, clearing the way before them by removing the stumbling-blocks, the rubbish of ages, which has been thrown upon it, and fencing it on each side, that in advancing toward the desired object they may not miss the way through mistake or inadvertency, by turning aside to the right hand or to the left, is, at least, the sincere intention of the above propositions. It remains with our brethren to say how far they go toward answering their intention. . . . If evidently defective . . . let them be corrected and amended, till they become sufficiently evident, adequate and unexceptionable. . . . If we have mistaken the way, we shall be glad to be set right; but if, in the meantime, we have been happily led to suggest obvious and undeniable truths which, if adopted and acted upon, would lead infallibly to the desired unity and secure it when obtained, we hope it will be no objection that they have not proceeded from a General Council'' (*Memoirs of Elder Thomas Campbell*, pp. 48-60). Mr. Campbell believed that ''union in truth'' had been and ever must be the desire of all who yearn for union, and that prayer must be resorted to and used.

The *Appendix* was added ''to prevent mistakes.'' Effort is made in it to answer possible objections, such as to purpose first of all. ''We beg leave to assure our brethren that we have no intention to interfere, either directly or indirectly, with the peace and order of the settled churches, by directing any ministerial assistance with which the Lord may please to favor us, to make inroads upon such, or by endeavoring to erect churches out of churches, to distract and divide congregations'' (*Memoirs of Elder Thomas Campbell*, p. 61). The place of creeds and confessions is touched upon; disavowal of wish or plan to be a party; the matter of disfellowshiping and latitudinarianism—which may be charged against the plan, come in for exposition.

It can not be successfully maintained that the materials and positions in the "Declaration and Address" are entirely original. Thomas Campbell had associated with men of thought and had been a great reader. Probably if he had taken time he could have cited from church fathers and reformers sentences and paragraphs similar to or containing the germ of his thought. The excellency of the Scriptures above mere men's deliverances, the authority of the Bible, the New Testament above and instead of the Old, the supremacy of the Lord Jesus Christ as to authority, the dependence of the church upon the testimony of the apostles, salvation by faith, the Christ and obedience to Him, the unity of the church and other subjects, some or all of which had engaged the attention of Irenæus (*Adv. Haer.*, 11, 27, 28; 13, 3, 4) and Origen (Fisher, *History of Christian Doctrine*, p. 105) among the ancients, and John Huss, Luther, Zwingli, Calvin, John Knox and John Wesley among the moderns. But they or their followers had not consistently followed out their findings and deliverances. There was an opening, so to speak, in the religious world of Thomas Campbell's day for a plea and a plan for Christian union. That the time was ripe for it, and that it was in the air, as it were, is to be seen by the efforts of the Haldanes in England and Scotland, Abner Jones in Vermont, James O'Kelly in Virginia and North Carolina, Barton W. Stone and his coadjutors in Kentucky.

Chapter X

FATHER AND SON JOIN FORCES

IN the month of October of 1809, at some place on the National Pike in Pennsylvania, there was a happy reunion of the Campbell family. Thomas and his son, Alexander, met after a separation of nearly two years. Both had changed during that time very materially in religious outlook, and surprised each other by confessions on the way. Father Campbell related his experiences with Chartiers Presbytery and the Associate Synod, and read to the son from the proof sheets of the "Declaration and Address." The younger man was delighted with what he heard, and expressed himself as ready to enter heartily into maintaining its positions before the world. It will be seen that the son had no share in shaping the document, but we are informed that he did press upon his father some of the things which he felt were logical conclusions from "Where the Scriptures speak, we speak; and where the Scriptures are silent, we are silent," and the propositions of the "Declaration and Address." The chief of these matters was in respect of infant baptism and immersion or the act of baptism.

Even though there was but one group meeting and one meeting-house, Thomas Campbell looked for the growth of the Christian Association and the need of a trained ministry. Therefore he began to train his own son in ministerial studies, and also set lessons for two other persons who showed some promise. Richardson relates (*Memoirs of Alexander Campbell,* Vol. I., p. 325ff.) that in the year 1810, some regular Presbyterians, ministers among them, urged upon Thomas Campbell that he make overtures to the Synod of Pittsburgh and try to make an "ecclesiastical union" with it. He agreed to an effort, and on October 14 he made his presentations. The petitioners spoke at length and answered some questions, but the Synod unanimously resolved not to receive him and his association. It also criticized the plan as one that would promote divisions, degrade ministerial character, provide for the free admission to any errors in doctrine and to any corruptions in discipline. Under the phrase which the Synod used in connection with its rejection, "Many other important reasons," lurked something that stirred Mr. Campbell. He understood that his character was in question, and so on the following day he appeared and asked the Synod the import of the phrase. He was furnished with the assurance that no question of immorality was involved, but matters about the confession of faith, and the impossibility, according to Presbyterian Church rules, of Synod's forming connection with any ministers, churches or associations. There were two other reasons that they assigned which are of particular interest. The first was, the Synod pointed out, the petitioner's inconsistency in declaring that the baptism of infants is not authorized by Scripture, precept or example, and is a matter of indifference, yet administering that ordinance while holding such opinion; and again, his temerity in encouraging or countenancing his son to preach the gospel without any regular authority (Richardson's *Memoirs*, Vol. I., p. 328).

What an unhappy lot was Thomas Campbell's at that time! A vision secured of a better state of the church, that it should have no divisions, and that creeds, main producers and perpetuators of divisions, should be relegated to an unauthoritative place! Yet with such vision his own original church refused to retain him. With such vision the Presbyterian Church refused to receive him. It was not in his heart to establish another sect or party. Existing parties would make no place for him, unless he smother his vision and begin to speak again the party shibboleths. The adherents of the Christian Association increased in number, and the building of a second meeting-house was called for. The reading of the "Declaration and Address" had not produced the results that its framer had hoped for. Instead of moving churches more toward unity and fellowship with others, it seemed to set them more fixedly in their disunity. That his plea for unity, brotherhood and tolerance was scriptural and of Christ, Mr. Campbell was thoroughly convinced. He could not renounce it except by beginning to walk in the darkness; nor could he be silent about it and be a good prophet of God. Consequently the way was not backward, but forward in hope. He was to learn that the uprooting of religious prejudices and the changing of religious bodies was not the task of a few months. It has been claimed by some students of the Restoration movement that if the son, Alexander, had not come upon the scene of activity at this time, the cause would have withered and died. Possibly so. Yet who knows? The course of the father up to this time had been one of energy and courage. He had stood without quailing before the princes of the church. He was in the prime of life. Why think that he would have changed and retired, just another disappointed soul? It is not to the father's discredit that he had a son of outstanding talent and of boundless energy who came to his aid in a great task, and who assumed, in a large degree, the direction of the effort at Christian union.

In 1811, Thomas Campbell left the town of Washington in which he had located his family, and established himself and them on a farm not far from Mt. Pleasant, where the second meetinghouse had been erected. On March 12 (before the removal from the town) he had lost from the family circle by marriage, his son Alexander, who had gone to live with his father-in-law on a farm near West Liberty, Va. As the time for the May meeting of the Christian Association drew on, a step that was undesirable, but seemingly inevitable, was prepared for. Paragraph IV. of the plans for that organization declared "That this society by no means considers itself a church, nor does at all assume to itself the powers peculiar to such

FATHER AND SON JOIN FORCES 129

a society, . . . but merely as voluntary advocates for church reformation.'' The events since October, 1809, and the attitude of church members to whose attention the thoughts and plans of the Christian Association were brought, convinced Thomas Campbell that the Association must resolve itself into a church. Accordingly this was done at the May meeting. The congregational type of organization was followed. Thomas Campbell was designated as elder, and four deacons were approved. The church issued to Alexander Campbell a license to preach. The elder at first betrayed his habit and training by seeking to use as a test of the faith and fitness of the members this question, ''What is the meritorious cause of a sinner's acceptance with God?'' This did not survive long. Weekly observance of the Lord's Supper began to be practiced. The failure of three persons who had been thought of as regular members, to partake brought to light the fact that they had not been baptized, and they were desirous of being immersed. After due consideration, Mr. Campbell agreed to do the immersing. On July 4, 1811, he plunged under the water two men and one woman, but not in the usual way. The pool was deep and overhung by a large tree. Upon the roots thereof Mr. Campbell stood as he said the words of the formula, and then submerged the heads of the candidates, for they were already immersed to their shoulders. Just as the Synod of Pittsburgh had charged him with inconsistency in performing infant baptisms in his present state of mind and teaching, so some members of the Brush Run Church charged him with failing in consistency when he immersed although not immersed. And in addition, his style of baptizing was the unaccustomed. This ordinance became the subject of more and more study in the church. It came home with inescapable force to the young traveling preacher, for so we must term Alexander at that time. He had been married on March 12, 1811, and on March 13, 1812, his wife had brought forth a daughter. What should he, they, do with respect to the infant—have her baptized or refrain from it? As never before, he took up the study of the question. The result was that he was entirely convinced that the right and permissibility of infant baptism were without authority in the Scripture, and, in addition, gained the sure conviction that scriptural baptism meant immersion only. This latter knowledge drove him to secure as soon as possible a baptism that would stand the test of the Scriptures. We must conclude that conversation and study about baptism had been going on in his father's home also. A sister, on the day when Alexander had come to inform his father and family about his newly gained conviction, spoke about her own dissatisfied mind, and feeling that she had never obeyed the Lord in baptism. He told his father and others that he was on the way to secure the Rev. Matthias Luce to baptize him. The father made no effort to intervene in the subject, only calling attention to what had been the attitude of the fellowship up to that time, and saying at the close, "You must please yourself." He did suggest that the son and the baptizing minister should call by on the day that they should set (Richardson's *Memoirs,* Vol. I., p. 395ff.). Was that the moment when the father capitulated in the matter of baptism? He never alluded to the day and hour so far as we have record, unless it was in the long sermon that he preached on the occasion of his baptism. The set day was June 12, 1812, and the place that which Thomas Campbell had already used as a baptistery. The greatest surprise of the day was that the father and his wife came with suitable changes of clothing. And the father took the lead in justifying his act in accepting what was new and had been up to that time a matter of indifference. It was a seven-hour service, and seven persons were immersed. It was novel also in that Alexander Campbell had stipulated that Mr. Luce should use the preposition "into" instead of the customary "in" in the formula, and that nothing but a simple confession of faith should precede. It was further well understood that they were not being baptized into the Baptist Church. A large concourse of people witnessed the baptisms and heard the sermons. The next Lord's Day thirteen other members of the Brush Run Church requested believers' baptism. In a short time that church became one of immersed believers, for those who did not receive immersion concluded that they belonged elsewhere. So baptism met those reformers as it had been meeting reformers from the first days of deviation from the scriptural declarations.

Luther, Zwingli, Calvin, Wesley, each and all had to face the subject of baptism. While they declared their beliefs as to the scriptural teaching, they made their decision so as to practice in conformity with existing creeds and current practice. The Campbells faced baptism and decided contrary to their old creed and current use. Without the Scriptures we might think that baptism was a device of the evil one to plague the church, to cause discussion and division among Christians, to turn thought from the inner things of the spirit to an external rite. Some believers have so treated it. But since baptism stands buttressed by language, the example of the apostles and the unmistakable command of the Head of the church, why should it not be looked upon as His device for union and spiritual blessing? It seems quite apparent to the writer that the Campbells, having taken the Scriptures as their sole rule of faith and practice, could not have done otherwise with respect to baptism.

Chapter XI

FELLOWSHIP WITH BAPTIST ASSOCIATION

IT is during the years of 1811 and 1812 that the son began to evidence his abilities as preacher and pleader of causes, and as a consequence less was said about his father. About this time also writers of the lives of the two men begin to pay less attention than deserved to the life of the father. Our endeavor is to atone for what may be termed a neglect. "The First Church of the Christian Association of Washington, meeting at Crossroads and Brush Run, Washington County, Pennsylvania" on January 1, 1812, chose and ordained Alexander Campbell as a minister thereof. But the fact was not documented until September 1, 1812, and was recorded legally in Brooke County, Virginia, at the December term of court. Thomas Campbell signed himself as "Senior minister"; the four deacons also affixed their signatures. What a mix-up that seems to be! One church with two meeting places. A champion of correct form and procedure would surely be astounded. Neither minister had been immersed at the time of the ordination; the church was not a Church of Christ nor a Christian Church. But it had not settled down with a creed that would bind its activities and hamper its thinking. It was as free as the Old and New Testament writings warranted it in being. Therefore we see it growing into a church after the pattern that is read of in the New Testament.

The Campbells, father and son, during 1812 and 1813, are found traveling and setting forth their views in western Pennsylvania, Ohio and Virginia, later named West Virginia. They made acquaintance with new people and churches. Especially were calls made for the son to address Baptists, and the fact that the Brush Run Church had become an immersionist group drew it closer to Baptist churches. No type of Presbyterianism promised a haven for these people who had become new by going back to the old. Dr. Errett Gates (*Early Relation and Separation of Baptists and Disciples*, p. 18ff.) writes "in many respects it [Brush Run Church] became a Baptist Church without the name during the year 1812." This the writer regards as unwarranted in an effort to show how close Baptists and those who later were called "Disciples" used to be. The records go to show that about the only respect in which Brush Run Church could qualify as a Baptist Church was in the act of baptism. It did not have the usual Baptist creed, the Philadelphia Confession of Faith; it had another church organization; it differed as to faith, regeneration, the place of the New Testament, the qualification for being baptized, the purpose of baptism, the frequency of communion, the relation of one church to another, and other matters that might be mentioned. Nevertheless, after much discussion on

FELLOWSHIP WITH BAPTIST ASSOCIATION 135

both sides as to the wisdom of entering into a formal relationship, the Redstone Baptist Association agreed to admit the Brush Run congregation as a fellowshiping church. The latter very distinctly indicated, however, that it was not becoming a Baptist Church, and expected perfect freedom "to teach and preach what they learned from the Holy Scriptures." A minority in the Association doubted the wisdom of the admission of Brush Run Church. It did prove to be a double-pointed thorn that pierced the sides of both Baptists and the adherents of "the new order of things." The copy of the document that set forth the terms of the communion with Redstone Association was asked of the clerk of the Association, and he refused it to the askers. But the sequel shows that the members of Brush Run Church did not violate the conditions of their entering the Association. It was well that no creed was adopted at the time, for both Thomas and Alexander Campbell were learning, and were sharing with the people their discoveries and conclusions. They for some three years maintained a correspondence with each other under the names "Philologus" (the father) and "Philamathes" (the son), and canvassed numerous interpretations of Scripture and ancient and modern ideas of religion. The members of the Brush Run Church were Christians. They had not taken the name of "Disciples" or "Reformers," and the opprobrious name "Campbellites" was about a decade off. Union with the Baptists took place in the fall of 1813, but rumblings among the Baptist preachers and churches indicated that it was not all the name implied.

One wonders whether Dr. Gates is entirely justified in his statement, "From this time Mr. (Alexander) Campbell regarded himself as a member of that denomination (the Baptist)." It is true that he was in and among them, but all things point away from his being a Baptist. He was not "of" the Baptists. I have seen in my studies no consciousness of Baptistism in either the father or son. Their teachings, outside the act of baptism, were in nothing confirmatory of Baptist positions of the times. What they preached as to the law, the covenants, the action of the Holy Spirit, creeds, faith, ordination, the church, were very much subversive of Baptist conceptions. It seems fair to say that they were tolerated in the Redstone Association for the fact that they were able to present the subject of immersion more skillfully and convincingly than any of the thoroughgoing Baptists. In 1815, the son Alexander wrote a letter to an uncle who was living in Ireland. It contained these significant words: "I am now an independent in church government; of that faith and view of the gospel exhibited in John Walker's *Seven Letters to Alexander Knox,* and a Baptist so far as regards baptism. Though my father and I accord in sentiment, neither of us are dictators or imitators. Neither of us lead; neither of us follow" (Richardson's *Memoirs,* Vol. I., p. 466ff.). To a group of ministers in Kentucky, in 1823, when he saw that they were receiv-

FELLOWSHIP WITH BAPTIST ASSOCIATION 137

ing him to their hearts because of his success in the debate with Mr. McCalla on the subject and form of baptism, Mr. Alexander Campbell said: "Brethren, I fear that if you knew me better, you would esteem me less. For let me tell you that I have almost as much against you Baptists as I have against the Presbyterians" (Richardson's *Memoirs*, Vol. II., p. 88). This seeming digression appears necessary to correct a rather current idea that the two Campbells had become quite Baptists. On the contrary, neither one ever felt under compulsion to hide from the Baptists, wherever they went preaching, any conviction as to truth, however contrary to the Baptist faith it might be. It is not to be wondered that some of the particular guardians of the Baptist ark felt that the Campbells were boring holes in their craft to its sinking. Some of the more narrow in the Redstone Association began to make efforts to oust those who had not come among them as Baptists. A quotation from an article in *The Christian Baptist* (Vol. 8, p. 160) indicates again Alexander Campbell's idea of himself (probably also of his father) in the Baptist Church: "Their (the Baptists) historian in the year 1900 may say, 'We are the only people who would tolerate, or who ever did tolerate, any person to continue as a reformer or as a restorer amongst us'."

For some reason, in 1813, Thomas Campbell resolved to enter the field as an educator. His son Archibald, in the sketch of his father (*Memoirs of Elder Thomas Campbell*, p. 123), states that about this time his father determined to advocate his cause without money and without price. The gift of a large, productive farm, by his father-in-law, had brought independence financially to Alexander Campbell. Did that fact quicken his father's desire to be less dependent upon his brethren for a living? "In pursuance of this grand purpose he, in the autumn of 1813, removed to Guernsey County, Ohio, within two miles of Cambridge, the county seat, where in connection with his farming operations, he opened an English Merantile Academy." The advocate of Christian union at the same time gave weekly addresses upon the Christian institution. Within two years he was in doubt about having found a proper location, although the school prospered. Towards the close of 1815 Mr. Campbell's old friend, General Acheson, of Washington, Pa., the same one who had signed the "Declaration and Address," and then had gone aside from its adherents, approached him in sore need. His brother, David Acheson, had become afflicted with a serious mental condition that rendered him difficult of restraint. For some reason the General believed that the presence and counsel of Thomas Campbell might have a salutary effect on his brother. There might have been some pique in the heart of Mr. Campbell over the defection of General Acheson, and he might have been minded to treat him as Paul did John Mark and Barnabas. However, he cherished no rancor nor bitterness. Sought for to perform an errand of mercy he turned the management of the school over to others, and went to Washington. For several weeks he was at the bedside of the ailing Mr. Acheson, and aided in every way until death released him from such confining service. During those weeks in Washington, Thomas Campbell learned that there was an opening for a mercantile academy in Pittsburgh. Some of his friends urged him to supply that need. What possibly moved him, above all, was that he saw an opportunity for a larger and more effective religious service than was possible in his present home in Ohio. Therefore he closed the institution near Cambridge, and started another in Pennsylvania's western metropolis. His family was able to assist in the instruction, and the school began to be a financial success.

We discover that in 1816 Mr. Campbell had constituted in Pittsburgh "a worshiping congregation upon the foundation of the apostles and prophets." At the meeting of the Redstone Baptist Association held at Cross Creek (Richardson's *Memoirs,* Vol. I., p. 480ff.), in 1816, during which A. Campbell preached the famous "Sermon on the Law," Thomas Campbell was present with a petition that is summed up under item 7 of the "Minutes of the Association": "7. A letter was presented by brother Thomas Campbell from a number of baptized professors in the city of Pittsburgh, requesting union as a church to this Association." Item 8 is of corresponding interest: "Voted that as this letter is not presented according to the constitution of this Association, the request cannot be granted."

It appears that Thomas Campbell had been appointed the previous year to present a circular letter on "The Trinity." While his church was refused admission as had been requested, Thomas Campbell was invited "to take a seat in this Association." He presented on the occasion the circular letter as had been assigned him, on "The Trinity." If it had been hoped to trap him into presenting the matter so that he might be condemned, he was too wise. The method of treatment that he adopted was so simple and devoid of the accustomed terminology and philosophical phrases, that for some reason it was accepted without question, and was printed at the close of the minutes. In case one is curious to read that "circular letter" on "The Trinity," in which the word "trinity" never occurs, he is referred to the Appendix to Volume I. of Richardson's *Memoirs*.

It must be noted that the Association appointed a committee to investigate the group that Mr. Campbell had gathered together in Pittsburgh, for there was already a group that consisted of eight persons in the same city that had standing as a church in the Association, a *Baptist Church,* for it had signed the usual covenant.

Chapter XII

FROM KENTUCKY BACK TO PENNSYLVANIA

IN the letter that Alexander Campbell had written on Dec. 28, 1815, to his uncle in Newry, occurs the sentence, "My father still resembles one of our planets in emigrating from place to place." He cites the three places—Washington, Cambridge and Pittsburgh. But it was too early to include the next place where his father sought to labor. The motive does not seem clear— Richardson suggests age and hope of service— but whatever it was, it carried Thomas Campbell down into Kentucky. In the early fall of 1817 he took his family to Newport, and spent some time looking into the lives of the people bordering on the Ohio. Ultimately he chose Burlington, county seat of Boone County, as his next home. It appeared a fine location for an English Classical Seminary. The residents were cordial, desired such an institution, and set about erecting the necessary building. The town was not provided with a church edifice, and therefore the Academy began to be used, on its completion, as a place for religious gatherings. Mr. Campbell was the preacher and used the method that had become common to him since his renunciation of the credal and scholastic method. The school prospered and began to attract pupils from a distance. The Kentuckians took the principal and his family to their hearts, and it began to appear that the peregrinations of the advocate of Christian union were at an end. There was not the highest satisfaction with the religious outlook, but regular meetings were maintained.

All classes of people attended. The majority were Baptists and of Baptist leaning. The message and methods of Thomas Campbell rather surprised the hearers, and the fruitage was small, even though large numbers heard (Richardson's *Memoirs*, Vol. I., p. 494ff.). In his new home Mr. Campbell had an opportunity of seeing slavery in its operations. He was stirred in heart to do something for the slaves. After having witnessed the way in which they spent Sunday afternoons he, on one occasion, invited them to come to his schoolroom and hear the reading of the Scriptures. They came with enthusiasm, heard earnestly, joined heartily in singing, and were promised on dismissal another such meeting soon. It was never repeated. The next day he was informed by one of his friends, of a state law that forbade any address to Negroes except in the presence of one or more white witnesses. He had broken the law but his friend assured him that no steps would be taken to prosecute him as he had been ignorant of the law. It was further urged that he have no more such meetings. Thomas Campbell was astonished, dumbfounded and well-nigh heartbroken. Quite speedily he resolved not to live where it was a crime to preach the gospel freely to any one;

where his family might be contaminated by the thoughts of those who approved the state's law and attitude. In a reply to a letter to his son Alexander, in which he had stated his dissatisfaction with the life in Kentucky and his intentions to remove therefrom, the father ascertained that there would be a place for him in Buffaloe Seminary. This school had been established two or three years before and was thriving. So back to Washington County, Pennsylvania, after about seven years of wandering, came Thomas Campbell; back where, in 1809, ten years before, he had given to the world a plea and plan for Christian union; back to renew fellowship with friends of former years; back to the region where he had suffered ostracism, misrepresentation, petty persecution and annoyance as he had gone about the business of teaching, preaching, visiting parishioners and baptizing converts (Richardson's *Memoirs*, Vol. I., p. 431); back to join his son in the growing work which was to see them co-operating happily until age and death claimed the father.

Locating his family on a farm about two miles from West Middletown, Pa., Thomas Campbell resumed pastoral care of the Brush Run Church, and assumed some of the instructing at Buffaloe Seminary, near the village of Bethany. These school duties necessitated his presence almost daily in the home of his son, where the school was quartered. The teaching abilities of both men were required in the prospering institution, but the call to travel more widely and preach, also to write, was heard by the son. He was beginning to suffer from overwork, and concluded to close the seminary in 1823. It had not fulfilled the desire of its founder in furnishing young men for the ministry (Richardson's *Memoirs,* Vol. II., p. 48).

In 1820 there seemed to be a departure from the plans of Thomas Campbell for the reformation, for an oral debate was held by his son with Rev. John Walker, at Mt. Pleasant, O., on the subject of baptism. He had hoped there would be no open controversy. He was not averse to written controversy. The two, father and son, had frequently exchanged letters as to their beliefs. The son had used the public press on several occasions to set forth his views, and to answer what were deemed false charges. Into that first debate Alexander Campbell was pushed with some reluctance. His father attended, possibly with some misgivings, and was called upon to dismiss the final session with prayer. The result was pleasing to both, because the hearing was large and the debate, for the most part, was orderly. From that time it was felt by the two that orderly discussion upon clearly stated propositions was a way by which the truth might be advanced. Thomas Campbell himself never engaged in an oral debate, but he was always interested in the debates of his son.

In 1820 occurred an event of great significance for the two churches of Christ interested in reform in religion—Brush Run and Bethany.* In the month of August, 1820, some of the more liberal

---

*Possibly this was just a meeting group.

Baptist churches of the Western Reserve of Ohio formed the Mahoning Baptist Association. The leader seemed to be Adamson Bentley. He had heard something about the novel teachings of the Campbells, had read the published record of the Campbell-Walker debate, which contained a very liberal appendix that sought to set people right as to certain false reports and slanders. In the summer of 1821 Mr. Bentley, together with Sidney Rigdon, visited Alexander Campbell at Bethany, and came away with the utmost confidence in his integrity and the correctness of his views (*Millennial Harbinger*, 1848, p. 523). More and more calls came for the father or son, or both, to visit various places in Ohio. They made it a practice to attend an annual meeting of the ministers of the Mahoning Association. But things were not moving in the Campbell's favor in the Redstone Association. A plan was concocted to disfellowship the two men and their fellows at the meeting in September, 1823. Special efforts had been made to have the churches appoint messengers who were unfriendly, especially to Alexander Campbell, whose famous "Sermon on the Law" was thought replete with heresy. Having been asked again and again to transfer their fellowship to the newer Association in Ohio, it was felt that rather than be ousted from the Redstone Association, Alexander Campbell would go out voluntarily. Because there seemed to be good reason for establishing a church of Christ at Wellsburg, on August 31, 1823, Alexander Campbell and thirty-one others were dismissed from Brush Run in good standing to form such a church, and the letter of dismissal was signed by Thomas Campbell (Richardson's *Memoirs,* Vol. II., pp. 68, 69). The younger Campbell was present at the Association meeting, but to the surprise of the heresy hunters he was not an appointed messenger. The meeting that had been packed to denounce and expel a heretic found itself without its big task. This turned the eyes and sympathies of the "reformers," as some began to call them, away from western Pennsylvania to Ohio as a better and more responsive field. In 1824, the Mahoning Association met at Hubbard and the church of Wellsburg sent three messengers with a request that their organization be admitted to membership. The clerk of the meeting wrote the following sixth item in his minutes: "At the request of the church of Christ at Wellsburg it was received into this Association." At that time the church which had been formed to thwart the scheme of Redstone Association leaders had grown to have forty members.

Chapter XIII

APOSTOLIC DOCTRINE BY PEN AND VOICE

THE counsel of three men in particular brought *The Christian Baptist* (Richardson's *Memoirs*, Vol. II., pp. 49, 50), a monthly periodical, into existence—Alexander Campbell, Thomas Campbell and Walter Scott. The last named was a young man of talent who was teaching and preaching in Pittsburgh. The first issue saw the light on July 4, 1823. The word "Baptist" was used as a carrier, for it was by no means intended to advocate Baptist principles in the magazine. In the words of the prospectus: "*The Christian Baptist* shall espouse the cause of no religious sect excepting that ancient sect, 'called Christians first at Antioch'." The father was not a frequent contributor, and then not under his own name, but under the initials "T. W." When "Editor" was seen, it was known that Alexander Campbell was speaking. Walter Scott chose "Philip" as his pen name. Until the close of 1829 this monthly went forth to be praised, cursed; treasured, burned; bring joy, cause sorrow; confirm churches, disturb churches; castigate the order of the clergy, encourage a ministry true and scriptural; expound the Scriptures and the ancient primitive faith, denounce and expose creeds, their teachings and effects; to teach a sane, scriptural influence of the Holy Spirit in conversion and sanctification, to show the folly of current ideas as to the Spirit's influence; to turn men into believers, disciples, Christians; to cause denominational and sectarian names to lose popularity and currency; to advocate oneness among Christians by following the New Testament model; to urge the abolition of existing religious establishments. The tone of *The Christian Baptist* was sometimes, if not often, a little too aggressive and denunciatory for the milder disposition of Thomas Campbell, and occasionally he injected an article or suggestion in a more irenic tone.

During those years after the closing of the seminary, he gave himself to traveling and preaching. Occasionally his name is found in reports in *The Christian Baptist;* more often his work was not heralded. His church was still in connection with the Redstone Association, but in 1826 a change came (Richardson's *Memoirs,* Vol. II., p. 163).

Under the guidance of champions of orthodoxy, led by Elder Brownfield, they constituted a minority representing ten churches as the true Association, and counted as heretical the other forty-two messengers from thirteen churches. One by one they were read out of the Baptist fold as guilty of being Arian, Socinian, Arminian, Antinomian, etc. Among the rejected was Brush Run Church and its messengers, one of whom was Thomas Campbell. The expelled messengers met in a near-by house and heard a sermon from Alexander Campbell, who was present as corresponding messenger of Stillwater and Mahoning Associations of Ohio. There was evidently some understanding among the messengers, for they went home and reported to the churches what had been done.

In November most of the expelled churches were represented at Washington, Pa., in the formation of a new Association of Washington. At the first meeting held on Sept. 7, 1827, a constitution was adopted which ignored the Philadelphia Confession, and had as its second article, "We receive the Scriptures as the only rule of faith and practice to all the churches of Christ." Was that simply the use of the name "churches of Christ" as belonging to even Baptist churches, or had they come along that far in abandoning sectarian phraseology? At this time the Brush Run Church was weakened by removals to such a degree that it seemed unwise to continue to meet. Consequently the remaining members, among whom were Thomas Campbell and his family, merged with the church that was organized near the home of Alexander Campbell.

In the autumn of 1827, father Campbell set forth to visit the leading churches on the Western Reserve. His companion was his youngest son, A. W. Campbell. The latter was making his debut as a public teacher and preacher. For some two months the two went among the churches, building them up and adding to the number of the saved. Again in the autumn of 1828, these emissaries of the ancient gospel directed their steps as far as Somerset County, Pa. They visited a few churches on the way as they found them in Washington, Fayette and Westmoreland Counties. At the county seat of Somerset, a town by the same name, they found in existence a small church whose main constituency was a group of women, who were remarkable for their intelligence and zeal. Their stay of three weeks was quite fruitful, for some thirty of the citizens of Somerset, most of the members of the bar, a physician and other men of education "became obedient to the faith."

The Mahoning Association was year by year advancing toward the position advocated by the Campbells, and in 1827 chose a traveling evangelist to visit among the churches and hold meetings (Richardson's *Memoirs,* Vol. II., p. 163ff.). Its choice was Walter Scott, then of Steubenville, and formerly of Pittsburgh, a teacher in Mr. Forrester's school, and one who had for some years been teaching the group of Christians that had responded to Mr. Forrester's influence. Scott was not a Baptist, except in immersion; was a great student of the Scriptures, and when he was called to evangelize was teaching in a seminary at Steubenville. He was about to begin publishing a monthly, which he proposed naming "The Millennial Herald." The call to evangelize was accepted, and Scott began what proved to be a very remarkable ministry among the Baptist churches. A knowledge of the same in the judgment of the writer warrants it to be included among classically entitled "Awakenings." Because his methods were so revolutionary, some church historians ignore or slur over Scott's ministry, but no small part of his method is seen in later evangelism, and even to this day.

He used the school children to advertise his meetings, sending them home to tell their parents to come out and hear a man preach the gospel on his five fingers (probably borrowing the idea from the five points of Calvinism). He adopted the plan of calling for immediate acceptance of Christ, and of urging men to be baptized for the remission of sins in the fashion and phrase of Peter on the day of Pentecost. Reformers and creeds had held all along that in baptism there was a sign and a seal of the remission of sins. Walter Scott used a singing evangelist, and found him very useful. The first year was a decided success. Scott's return to the methods used in the Book of Acts not only stirred up sinners, but also preachers, and the latter began to preach in like manner. The annual meeting of Mahoning Association in the following year showed that hundreds had been added to the churches, whereas eleven churches had reported in the previous year thirty-four added by baptism, and several churches had no additions at all. The details of those meetings showed that men and women were moved to tears and joy, and prayer abounded.

News of the great harvest of souls on the Western Reserve of Ohio reached the Campbells in Bethany. They were filled with wonder and anxiety. Was Walter Scott being carried away by over-enthusiasm? Was he preaching and practicing some other thing than that they had thought to be the ancient gospel? It was decided that Thomas Campbell should visit the Reserve, go among the churches and get into contact with Mr. Scott. "The venerable Thomas Campbell saddled his favorite sorrel and made an extensive tour of these battlefields. . . . Nothing could have been more opportune; just such a man was needed; and none who never saw him can well appreciate the great effect of the presence, counsels and addresses of this noble man. Uniting the simplicity of a child with the dignity of a senator, agreeable almost to playfulness, with a piety so pure, sweet and unostentatious as to command the respect and admiration of all around him, the newly formed churches felt in his presence the timely aid, encouragement and counsel which could be imparted by no other one so well. His fame and ability as a scholar and as a speaker drew large audiences" (Hayden, *Early History of Disciples on the Western Reserve*). He found that Walter Scott could contribute something to him as he acknowledges in this extract from a letter to Alexander, his son: "We have spoken and published many things *correctly* concerning the ancient gospel—its simplicity and perfect adaptation to the present state of mankind, for the benign and gracious purposes of its immediate relief and perfect salvation—but I must confess that in respect of the direct exhibition and application of it for that purpose, I am, at present, for the first time, upon the ground where the thing has appeared to be practically exhibited to the proper purpose. 'Compel them to come,' saith the Lord, 'that my house may be filled.' Mr. Scott has made a bold push to accomplish this object, by simply and boldly stating the ancient gospel and insisting upon it; and then by putting the question generally and particularly to males and females, old and young: 'Will you come to Christ and be baptized for the remission of your sins and the gift of the Holy Spirit? Don't you believe this blessed gospel? Then come away,' etc., etc. This elicits a personal conversation; some confess faith in the testimony—beg time to think; others consent—give their hands to be baptized as soon as convenient; others debate the matter friendlily; some go straight to the water, be it day or night, and upon the whole none appear offended.'' This visit of the great apostle of Christian union seems to have lasted from April until the fall meeting of the Mahoning Association. He traveled extensively and labored abundantly, preaching publicly and exhorting from house to house. His influence was salutary and inspiring upon older and younger preachers to whom he was Barnabas reborn. Among those whose lives he touched and blessed at this time were Reuben Ferguson, a Methodist preacher, who, upon embracing the ancient faith, began to preach it; and Aylett Raines, a Restorationist. He was able to lead the latter into preaching a certain, blessed gospel for the present life, and the two traveled and evangelized together for several months. When some would have driven Raines from the fellowship, because of his former faith, the elder Campbell stood by him and held that as long as Aylett Raines believed, accepted and obeyed Christ, he could have what opinions he pleased provided he did not preach them. Especially in the Western Reserve were people from all sects with their opinions being gathered into the churches and how to be one was their problem. If Methodists, Restorationists, Universalists, New Lights, Baptists were to advocate their old (and possibly present) opinions on matters that were basic to their old system, there was no gain. But if all would cleave to the things of the faith which rests upon the testimony of the apostles, then they could be united. When the case of Mr. Raines was up, Thomas Campbell said: "Brother Raines and I have been much together for the last several months, and we have mutually unbosomed ourselves to each other. I am a Calvinist, and he a Restorationist; and although I am a Calvinist, I would put my right arm into the fire and have it burned off before I would raise my hand against him. And if I were Paul, I would have Brother Raines in preference to any other young man of my acquaintance to be my Timothy" (*Early History of the Disciples*, etc., p. 168). At the 1828 meeting of the Mahoning Association, after hearing Walter Scott's report and disposing of the question of the bounds of his labors, he was re-engaged, but with William Hayden as singer and exhorter. Scott had said: "Brethren, give me my Bible, my head and Bro. William Hayden and we will go out and convert the world." In that very fashion he was engaged for the ensuing year.

Chapter XIV

SOCIALISM—MILLENNIALISM—MORMONISM

THE debate with Robert Owen, of England, infidel philanthropist and colonizer, took place in Cincinnati, O., in 1830. He had paid a short visit to the Campbells at Bethany the previous year and had learned to prize the manliness of both Alexander Campbell and his father. The latter went with his son to the city of the debate, and was present throughout the eight days of its progress, from April 13 to April 21. He remained in Cincinnati for several days after the departure of the principals, and baptized several converts. Dr. Richardson writes that Mr. Owen was greatly impressed with the "urbanity, kindness and many excellent qualities of the elder Campbell."

Thomas Campbell was present in Kentucky at the Elkhorn Baptist Association meeting in 1830, when the churches at Versailles, Providence and South Elkhorn were excluded from fellowship in order to reach some prominent Baptists who were advocates of the primitive faith and order. In 1828, Thomas Campbell and Alexander had been present in the Stillwater Baptist Association in Ohio, when Cyrus McNeely was tried for having baptized a convert at the Cadiz Church over which he was presiding and before he had been ordained. The Campbells defended the course of the young baptizer as perfectly scriptural. The complexion of the churches composing the Mahoning and Stillwater Associations had so altered in the preceding years that in 1830 they both ceased as Associations and resolved themselves into annual meetings that provided for the complete autonomy of the individual churches.

The years 1825 to 1830 were those of the greatest defection from Baptist churches to the ranks of the "Reformers" (*Early History of the Disciples*, etc., p. 168). Some time during those years "Campbellites" arose as a rude term of reproach for those who sought to follow the New Testament only. Ohio and Kentucky were especial fields of labor for Thomas Campbell during the indicated years. An extract from a letter written to his wife on Aug. 30, 1830, reveals something of his travels, thoughts and outlook. He had been absent from home for six months in 1829 in the Western Reserve, and would complete another six months of absence in Kentucky before returning to his home. He noted that since his marriage he had been one-seventh of the time away from his home and family, and craved that his wife would forgive him that wrong. "I have not enjoyed so even and so confirmed a state of health these many years. Notwithstanding the heat and drouth and dust, and my almost daily speaking, from two to three hours at a time, I have not had so much as a headache since I left home. . . . I can give you no adequate idea of the weight and heat of the work in Kentucky. The outrageous and malevolent opposition is ripening the harvest for the reformers. A. Campbell, Campbellism, Campbellites and heretics are the chorus, the overword, the tocsin of alarm in the mouths of the opponents—in almost every sentence from the one end of Kentucky to the other; yea, in the opposition and in the papers from Georgia to Maine. You can not conceive what a terrible dust our humble name has kicked up. If it were not coupled with the pure cause of God— the ancient gospel of the Saviour, and the sacred order of things established by his holy apostles, I should tremble for the consequences! But alas! the enemies have blasphemed the blessed gospel by pasting our sinful names upon it, to bring it into disrepute" (*Memoirs of Elder Thomas Campbell*, pp. 151, 152). The tone of this letter shows he had not swerved from the positions of the Declaration and Address taken more than twenty years before, and that he was ready to accept what came as long as he was loyal to the Lord.

Three significant things happened in the religious world in 1830. The first was an unusual agitation of the subject of the millennium. Walter Scott had cast his annual report to the Mahoning Association in 1828 in millennial terminology. Two works on prophecy, one by Elias Smith and another by James Begg, had stirred Scott. Other preachers were catching up something of Scott's message and anticipation of the millennium. The second significant thing was the establishment of *The Millennial Harbinger* to take the place of *The Christian Baptist*. In that monthly it was intended to treat a wider range of subjects, "and to show 'the inadequacy of modern systems of education,' and the *injustice* yet remaining 'under even the best political governments' in regard to various matters connected with the public welfare" (Richardson's *Memoirs,* Vol. II., p. 303). Moreover, it gave place to the discussion of the millennium and the second coming. Alexander Campbell, under a pseudonym "The Reformed Clergyman," reviewed the articles, striving to correct the errors therein and to keep men from turning away from the practical work of the gospel. It is a tribute to the sanity of both the Campbells that neither one embraced the extravagant hopes of the times nor felt that any theory of the millennium was an essential part of the gospel. The third thing was the beginning of the Mormon delusion. Sidney Rigdon had become somewhat affected by Walter Scott's warm advocacy of the early onset of the millennium, and he became a tool for those who sought to impose on the world a new religion with a new revelation. It may be that Mr. Rigdon was smarting under the rejection of a proposed scheme of communism for the churches, and saw a way to honor through Mormonism. Joseph Smith had a revelation for Mr. Rigdon that characterized him as a John the Baptist. The Mormon message was launched in the heart of the Western Reserve of Ohio, and had its first hearing among Baptists and churches of Christ.

The venerable Thomas Campbell, who already had a great many children of the faith in that region, hearing of the defection of Sidney Rigdon and the progress that the delusion was making, left his Bethany home and came into the center of the new battle. He spent much time of the winter of 1830 and 1831 in Mentor and vicinity. His wise counsels and great weight of influence interposed an effectual barrier to Mormonism's encroachments. From Mentor, O., on Feb. 4, 1831, he addressed a letter to Mr. Rigdon from which we quote some sentences and paragraphs: "It may seem strange, that instead of a confidential and friendly visit, after so long an absence, I should thus address, by letter, one whom for many years I have considered not only as a courteous and benevolent friend, but as a beloved brother and fellow-laborer in the gospel; but, alas! how changed and fallen! Nevertheless I should now have visited you, as formerly, could I conceive that my so doing would answer the important purpose, both to ourselves and to the public, to which we both stand pledged, from the conspicuous and important stations we occupy—you as the professed disciple and public teacher of the infernal Book of Mormon, and I as the professed disciple and public teacher of the supernal books of the Old and New Testaments of our Lord and Saviour Jesus Christ, which you now say is superseded by the Book of Mormon—is become a dead letter; so dead that the belief and obedience of it, without the reception of the latter, is no longer available for salvation. To the disproof of this assertion, I understand you to defy the world. . . . . I, therefore, as in duty bound, accept the challenge, and shall hold myself in readiness, if the Lord permit, to meet you publicly, in any place, either in Mentor or Kirkland, or in any of the adjoining towns that may appear most eligible for the accommodation of the public. The sooner the invistigation takes place the better for all concerned.

"The proposition that I have assumed, and which I mean to assume and defend against Mormonism and every other *ism* that has been assumed since the Christian era, is the all-sufficiency of the Holy Scriptures of the Old and New Testaments, vulgarly called the Bible, to make every intelligent believer wise to salvation, thoroughly furnished for any good work. This proposition, clearly and fully established, as I believe it most certainly can be, we have no more need for Quakerism, Shakerism, Wilkinsonianism, Buchmanism, Mormonism, or any other ism, than we have for three eyes, three ears, three hands, or three feet, in order to see, hear, work or walk." In the rest of the letter Mr. Campbell specifies special propositions to which he will address his argumentation, six of them dealing with the claims of Mormonism. Hayden states: "Mr. Rigdon read a few lines of this communication and then hastily committed it to the flames" (*History of the Disciples,* pp. 217-220). It was about a year later (March, 1832) that Joseph Smith and Sidney Rigdon were taken from the headquarters of Mormonism and tarred and feathered. We may be sure that Thomas Campbell had no part in that questionable proceeding, for the perpetrators were citizens of Shalersville, Garrettsville and Hiram, who had discovered the certainty of the fraud and resented the way in which they had been duped.

Chapter XV

NAME—NEW NEW TESTAMENT—BEREAVEMENT

THINGS were not always peaceful in the young churches of the reformation. On several occasions, elders, preachers and churches sent for Thomas Campbell to restore order and Christian fellowship. F. W. Emmons refers to one such occasion in connection with the church at New Lisbon, O., in 1831. "I then felt that the testimony of Luke for Barnabas might well be applied to him (father Campbell), that 'he was a good man and full of the Holy Spirit and faith.' Yes, he was good, he was devout, and with Edwards and Judson and Payson he ascribed all his goodness to the grace of God." Mr. Emmons assures us, too, that Thomas Campbell "was like Paul in withstanding and reproving error." This he heard him do once in Wellsburg. An effort was being made by a young preacher there to convince his hearers that "the Spirit was the Word and the Word was the Spirit." After terminating his discourse, before the preacher had time to dismiss the audience, "Father Campbell arose, with the dignity and solemnity of a patriarch, as he was, and spoke for some ten or fifteen minutes in reply. Ah, with what force and plainness for the truth! and yet, with tenderness and kindness for the young man." It will be recalled that there were some who charged that Alexander Campbell was the author and maintainer of the teaching referred to above. May we be allowed to insert here a few words drawn from the mind of Alexander Campbell as he comments on the circumstance related by Mr. Emmons? "The case of the young preacher is suggestive. Ardent, inexperienced, and fond of paradox, the recklessness, which is often mistaken for manly courage, to avoid a vicious extreme, he ran into its opposite, no less prejudicial to truth and righteousness—an event which is due to an unsettled state of the public mind. To relieve himself from views of spiritual influence which negative human responsibility, he made religion merely mechanical. Unread in the controversy, he accepted an extreme view which seemed to void all the difficulties of the subject. Doubtless Father Campbell's eclaircissement of the theme and our young friend's subsequent readings of the living oracles, led him, by a just exegesis of these Scriptures, to form more scriptural and spiritual views of his religion, and, we would fain hope, enjoy it in proportion to the increase of light" (*Memoirs of Thomas Campbell*, pp. 282, 283).

It is an admirable comment on the independence of mind possessed by both, to observe that father and son did not always and entirely agree as to teachings and the advisability of published writings. They did agree on the great fundamental elements of faith, but in opinions each allowed the other latitude. The matter of the name for the new type of followers of Christ necessarily presented itself. Barton W. Stone and his associates in the Kentucky region brought a revival of the name "Christian" which had so largely been discarded because of a predilection for denominational and sectarian names. To that name "Christian" Thomas Campbell leaned as the best. His son became persuaded that "disciple" was better, inasmuch as it was older in the Scriptures, was more humble and had not been appropriated. They did not quarrel in the matter of name, but each used what he pleased, and both men used both names. Once the young editor of *The Millennial Harbinger* had written the "Dialogue on the Holy Spirit," in which he had employed abstractions and philosophical distinctions in relation to "moral and physical powers," with a view to make himself, he said, "understood, but which really opened the way to new misunderstandings. . . . " Thomas Campbell quite disapproved of the dialogue as a full and just presentation of the subject. The dialogue had been included in a first edition of "Christianity Restored." In deference to the opinion of his father, the son omitted the questioned article from a subsequent edition of the book (Richardson's *Memoirs of Alexander Campbell,* Vol. II., pp. 354, 355). Only the two men knew how much each served as a check and balance upon the other.

In December of 1831, Thomas Campbell made a tour of the churches in Virginia. He had numerous contacts with adherents of the reformation that were to be found in nearly all of the Baptist churches. There were those who were glad to hear more of the teachings and proposals for union and restoration, and, of course, there were others who were bitter and endeavored to turn their fellows away from the teaching and Mr. Campbell. The stay was prolonged into 1832. Even the irenic temper and method of the advocate of Christian union availed not to avert division in several of the churches.

Into the arena of the religious life of the United States in 1826 Alexander Campbell sent forth a new edition of the New Testament. It was really a work of Drs. George Campbell (not a relative), James MacKnight and Philip Doddridge. It had been well received in the British Isles, even though it paid scant respect to some of the old texts in the King James Version, that had been used to bolster Calvinism and Arminianism. It even conceded that the term "baptism" ought to be replaced in religious literature and the Scriptures by "immersion." Its new publisher sent it forth with a preface, various emendations and an appendix. What a furore this work caused! It was the "Campbellite Bible" even though it deserved rather the title, the "Presbyterian Bible." The first edition was soon exhausted, and a second was called for and evidently published, though there seems to be no record of it. The preface to the third edition opens as follows: "Six years have transpired since we published the first edition of this work. During this period we have been receiving criticisms, suggestions and queries, relative to further improvements in the version and in the mode of exhibiting it.

We also solicited and obtained, from some learned and pious men their assistance in perfecting this translation." None of these are mentioned by name. Then there was a praiseworthy plan to issue a pocket edition of the New Testament, a "stereotype edition." The second paragraph of the preface to that issue reads in part: "Aware of all the difficulties in our way, and most solicitous to have the stereotype pocket edition of this work as perfect in its typography as any in existence, we have been at the labor and expense of preparing two editions at one and the same time—so that any errata discovered after the sheets of the third edition were worked off, might be corrected in the standing form of the pocket edition." And now the third paragraph of the aforementioned "Preface to the Fourth, or Stereotype Edition": "The sheets of the third edition, after having been read repeatedly by myself and others, were submitted to the examination of Thomas Campbell, Sen., and of Francis W. Emmons, to whom we are much indebted for the care which they have bestowed on them, and the numerous suggestions with which they have favored us. Their classical and biblical attainments have been of much service to us and to the public, in the completion of this work." A very justifiable tribute of not only youth to age, but of one scholar to another, Alexander Campbell, junior, to Thomas Campbell, senior. There never was a more conscientious effort put forth to have a humanly perfect copy of the writings of the New Covenant. An extract from a long letter written by the father to his son concerning the state of the cause in Virginia touches the above translation work. The date is Aug. 1, 1832, Spotsylvania, Va., the place, and the sentiment the following: "I think long, my dear son, to be at home, not only for the sake of my family enjoyment, but, in a peculiar measure, for the sake of a final revision of your intended impression of the New Testament. Were this satisfactorily accomplished, I should be comparatively at ease about other achievements. It was with great reluctance I left home on that account. If the Lord be graciously pleased to spare my unworthy life to see this thing happily accomplished, I shall greatly rejoice in his goodness, through his special grace. May the Lord bless and prosper his precious word that it may be light, life and joy to a guilty and erring world." And both father and son were committed to the idea that the Scriptures ought to be translated so as to give the mind of the Spirit back of its giving. It requires no stretch of the imagination to believe that the elder Campbell acquiesced in the deliverance of the younger which is found at the close of the first preface, which is dated Jan. 29, 1826: "I do most solemnly declare, that, as far as respects my feelings, partialities, reputation and worldly interest as a man, I would become a Presbyterian, a Methodist, a Quaker, a Universalist, a Socinian, or anything else before the sun would set today, if the apostolic writings would, in my judgment, authorize me in so doing; and that I would not give one turn to the meaning of an adverb, preposition or interjection to aid any sectarian cause in the world. Whether every reader may give me credit in so declaring myself I know not; but I thought it due the occasion thus to express the genuine and unaffected feelings of my heart. May all who honestly examine this version abundantly partake of the blessings of that Spirit which guided the writers of this volume, and which in every page breathes 'Glory to God in the highest heaven, peace on earth, and good will among men'."

Our data are quite meager as to the relations of our "Advocate of Christian Union," and the followers of Barton W. Stone and his colaborers. Their converts had spread into Ohio and farther west. There are occasional references to the Christians of the Stone type in the regions of Ohio, where the older Campbell preached and evangelized. In 1824, Alexander Campbell and Mr. Stone met in Kentucky, and from that time they had a warm regard for each other. They saw a great similarity in the message and the main task of each other. They read each other's writings and sought to help each other into the larger truth. But not until the early '30s did the groups of "Reformers" or "Disciples" and "Christians" begin to get together in appreciable degrees. Much is owed such preachers as Samuel Rogers, John Gano, John T. Johnson, John Smith and John Rogers. The union of the important churches in Georgetown, Lexington and Paris stirred the two groups in the entire state of Kentucky to unite and there was great joy in most hearts. There was a group of the adherents of the Stone movement that sharply criticized the action of Mr. Stone, but he said: "This union, irrespective of reproach, I view as the noblest act of my life" (*History of the Disciples*, p. 120). The name of Thomas Campbell does not seem to figure in the union spoken of, but he felt called upon to conduct a sort of magazine debate with Mr. Stone on the subject of "The Atonement." There were many who doubted that Mr. Stone was sound and completely scriptural in his views. In four installments in *The Millennial Harbinger*, (*Millennial Harbinger*, pp. 493ff., 503ff., 548ff., 594ff.), the elder Campbell set forth his ideas and made strictures on what he thought were the defective views of the Kentucky reformer. The first writing appeared in Volume III., 1833. As people understood him, they thought that Mr. Stone seemed to be satisfied with a moral theory of the atonement. His reviewer sought to show that, while the moral theory was not wrong, it did not satisfy all the teachings of the Scriptures on the subject. There was no denunciation, but an earnest desire and hope that each one might attain to the full truth.

In 1833 the two Campbells and three other companions set forth on a horseback tour of Virginia and the East. They traveled together as far as Richmond, and, after some time in that city, they separated—Alexander to go on north as far as New York, the father turning south into North Carolina. The latter was more than seventy years of age at the time, and just as earnest as ever in his advocacy of the principles of the "Declaration and Address." His desire was for peace among the churches and forbearance in love, but he saw and heard sorrowful things. The "Dover Decrees" had crossed from Virginia into the Carolinas, and were being read and circulated among the Baptist churches. During his visit he saw the Yeopim Union Meeting formally excluding the group of "Disciples" in the church of Edenton. A committee was appointed and called "The Committee on the Case of the Campbellite Reformers." This body made its report in three resolutions, the third being to the effect that it is "due to the cause of truth and Christian concord to guard our brethren against the ministrations of the one, Thomas Campbell, a teacher of Campbellism, who has been for some time visiting among our brethren, carrying with him letters of recommendations from persons residing in Edenton, and laboring, it is believed, to disseminate his peculiar sentiments among our people." So outrageous were the reports about him and his mission that Mr. Campbell felt called to issue a pamphlet in reply and self-defense. There were places, however, during his prolonged stay of six months in North Carolina where he was gladly received, and he had joy in his ministry (Vare, *Disciples of Christ in North Carolina*, p. 59ff.).

A preaching and lecturing tour of seventy-five days' duration, turned the editing of *The Millennial Harbinger*, for several of the early months of 1835, over to the elder Campbell. The regular editor (Alexander Campbell) had left some articles for insertion, but the editor-ad-interim did considerable writing also. A letter from J. R. Howard touching the sufferings of Christ and the relations of the act of baptism to the same drew forth a rather extended reply. Thomas Campbell answers a series of six questions, the last of which was, "Is baptism a church ordinance?" There had been manifested "the editorial itch" among many converts to, and adherents of, the "Reformation" with the result that many magazines sprang up in various quarters. Both of the Campbells, although they felt many of those journalistic efforts were ill-advised, manifested no jealousy and gave due notice of the competitors, in some respects, in the *Harbinger*. Not only in some of those new magazines and papers, but also in some pulpits, was attention being given to "untaught questions," "vain philosophies" and heresies, both ancient and modern. Such writings and preachments were a grief of mind to the originator of the plan for Christian union, and during the period now under review, he wrote as follows: "Had the advocates of the proposed reformation continued to sustain and enforce it (the abundant and alone sufficiency of the Holy Scriptures) as in the document referred to [the "Declaration and Address"], we are constrained to believe that the sectarian popular objections which have been brought against it, and with which its progress has been unhappily embarrassed, could never have been advanced by any who acknowledged the all-sufficiency and alone-sufficiency of the belief and obedience of the Holy Scriptures in the obvious grammatic sense, for the salvation of sinners, for the perfect edification of the Christian church, independent of all human opinions and inventions of men. . . . Thus instead of a genuine scriptural reformation reducing and restoring our holy religion to its original heaven-born purity, in the belief and practice of a divine declaration, expressly upon the face of the sacred page, we should have a reiteration, a renewed exhibition of metaphysical abstractions, of theological polemics, notions and opinions to which Buck's *Theological Dictionary* might again serve as a portable index. *Ainsi ne soit il.*" Again: "If we calculate the future by the past, especially the last ten years, we might live to see an exhibition of all the curious questions and controversies of the last fifteen centuries upon the page of the periodicals professedly in favor of the proposed reformation." At this time, Thomas Campbell and wife were living with a son-in-law and the daughter Jane, the McKeevers, near West Middletown, Pa.

In 1835, Mrs. Campbell was taken with what proved to be a fatal illness. Her husband was constantly at her bedside, and they had much intimate fellowship in the things of their common faith. Her remains were laid to rest in the family burying-ground at Bethany. The aging widower wrote a very human account of the last illness and death of his wife to the daughter Alicia (Mrs. Matthew C. Clapp), who was living in Ohio. The same letter was inserted in the *Harbinger*. Reference was made by the bereaved father to the fact that in the last eight years his wife had been deprived of his company three-fourths of the time. He confessed that in the years of their almost fifty of wedded life, his wife had carried the heavy load of nurturing and training the children and keeping the home. But she had agreed to be a sharer with him in his life's work, and that called for her to share him with a world which he felt needed his message. Herewith the closing paragraph of the obituary letter: "And now, dear daughter, what remains for me thus bereft of my endearing, attached companion, from whose loving, faithful heart, I am persuaded, I was not absent a single day of our fifty years' connection —yes, what now remains for me without any worldly care or particular attachment, but with renewed energy, with redoubled diligence, as the Lord may graciously be pleased to enable, to sound abroad the *word* of life."

Chapter XVI

A WATCHFUL EYE ON THE REFORMATION

FOR several years we have little data remaining to show how this rededication to his task was fulfilled. In 1836, Dr. Robert Richardson was induced to remove to Bethany to become associate in the publication of the *Harbinger*. This gave more freedom to both the Campbells. A general outline of the activities of Alexander is kept before us in the magazine, but we catch only an occasional glimpse of the father. In 1836, "My Dear Son" published a rather extensive letter from his father which dealt with devotion to the original idea of the reformation and the importance of giving to all who professed adherence to it a correct understanding of the same.

Debates with the Baptists in periodicals and in sermons, reached such proportions, sometimes the Reformers leading and then the Baptists, that in the year 1835, Alexander Campbell, in the *Harbinger,* proposed that "the Baptists select some one to write a tract of sixty or one hundred pages in defence of their system, assailed by us, and we will furnish like pages in support of our views and in exposure of theirs, the same to be published and circulated widely so that papers be left free for other things." That proposal surely pleased the elder Campbell, but nothing came of it. The discussions by pen and tongue continued with the Baptists, but other faiths were given attention. In 1836 occurred the memorable discussion with the Roman Catholic Bishop Purcell (later elevated to an archbishopric). So exhaustively did the editor of *The Millennial Harbinger* examine and discuss Roman Catholicism that the Roman Catholic authorities take no satisfaction in the distribution of the printed report of the discussion. The elder Campbell seems not to have been present at the debate. In the same year a discussion with a Mr. Skinner on the merits of Universalism was conducted in the *Harbinger,* and it lasted for almost two years. An incidental note in an 1838 *Harbinger* states that the circulation of the various issues of the New Testament prepared by the Campbells had reached about 24,000. In the same year Dr. Richardson wrote a letter from Hillsborough, Va., to "Beloved old brother T. Campbell: Learning from brother Alexander when he was at my house, you would attend to the *Harbinger*, I address you as the Editor." How long the absence of the editor gave him that honor then we are not sure.

In 1839, from the "old brother," came an article on "The Divine Order for Evangelizing the World, and for Teaching the Evangelized How to Conduct Themselves." He started with the Great Commission in Matthew, and urged the necessity of teaching and preaching. "Let the church then take up its Book and read and study it. The proper character of the church is the school of

Christ, disciples, Christians. . . . It must not shame its Master by its stupid, wilful, shameful ignorance of His Book." He proposed for the Lord's Day a meeting of four hours, beginning at ten o'clock and a half-hour intermission between each two hours. An order of service is really suggested which provides at the close for assignments of study for the week and "a contribution of something to the common stock for religious purposes, as God has prospered him." A record book was proposed for each church that should have "1. A declaration of sentiment. 2. The names of the members. 3. A record of additions by baptism, by letter, or otherwise [we use this very method of recording additions today]. 4. A record of deaths; also of dismissals, specifying the time and causes. 5. An account of contributions and expenditures." This article was followed by a series entitled "Church Edification," and still another named "A Scriptural View of Christian Character and Privileges" (five articles). These productions indicate that the elder Campbell was concerned for the well-being of the new churches that were springing up everywhere. In 1839 (*Millennial Harbinger*, p. 19) we see Thomas Campbell ranging himself with Barton W. Stone in favor of using the name "Christian" and against Alexander Campbell, who had announced himself in favor of using the name "Disciple," though not exclusively. Again in the following year the father published a short article in which he maintained that the name "Christian" was to be preferred.

"First, because of the radical and comprehensive import of its appellative signification. Second, because of its scriptural consistency with the intention of the proposed reformation."

Toward the close of 1838 and the opening of 1839, the attention of our "advocate of Christian union" was challenged by a Christian Union Convention, which held its first session in Syracuse, N. Y., and its second in Cazanovia, N. Y. This seems to have been the first formal effort at Christian union since Thomas Campbell's publication of the Declaration and Address in 1809. There had been associated denominational activity for work among the Indians. Mr. Campbell did not attend, but took his knowledge of the convention through articles in the *Union Herald*. Three installments of the reports are spread on the pages of the *Harbinger* by way of acquainting all with the new proposal for the union of Christians. There was a report of a committee on resolutions, which presented what it thought were fundamental propositions that all should adhere to. There were several addresses which magnified the object and the immediate necessity of the same. There was some discussion which revealed that theological agreement was thought to be the way into unity. Possibly the reply of Thomas Campbell will be sufficient to indicate the nature of the propositions and the prevailing thought of that Christian Union Convention. "Having presented to the readers of the *Harbinger* in this and two preceding numbers a large and comprehensive extract of the proceedings and sentiments of a respectable number of ministers and others, principally of the state of New York, in convention assembled at Syracuse, Aug. 21, A. D. 1838, and at Cazenovia, Jan. 30 and 31, 1839, for the desirable purpose of Christian union, we now proceed to make some remarks upon the said documents.'' He expressed his joy in the fact that this all-important subject is beginning to awake the public. ''Some thirty years ago, when we addressed a portion of our fellow Christians in western Pennsylvania upon this all-important subject, we met with universal opposition from the leaders of the people and were considered as the disturbers of religious society; but now, blessed be God, it is not only our privilege to hear of some hundreds of thousands in the United States and elsewhere that have been awakened, by means of our humble commencement, to advocate this blessed cause, upon pure scriptural principles of primitive, apostolic Christianity; but that also now, at length, there is a voluntary movement in different parts of the camp, beyond the bounds of our co-operative agency, in favor of this blessed cause, the cause of *union in truth amongst all the friends of truth and peace throughout all the churches,* for this was the sacred design and motto of our commencement.'' Here he cites propositions 1, 8, 9, 10, 11, 12, 5 and 3 in this order. ''Adopting and acting upon these principles, as apparently the only just and scriptural alternative for the multifarious corruptions and divisions which have desolated and ruined the Christian church, we have reason to rejoice that our humble commencements have been crowned with a degree of success far exceeding our most sanguine expectations; and which we believe nothing but the divine approbation could have effected; for we have been most bitterly and vehemently opposed by the leaders of all parties—Atheistic, Deistic, Catholic and Protestant—with which we have happened to come in contact. But, blessed be God, in spite of all opposition, the good cause of scriptural reformation is happily prevailing; and no doubt will continue to do so, till all anti-Christian errors and corruptions be forever abolished.

"Second, as to the propositions adopted by the convention, they appear too indefinite, and, of course, have a tendency to produce difficulties, both to the candidates for Christian fellowship, and also to those who are to admit and receive them. We mean the first and second propositions that were adopted by the convention in their former meeting at Syracuse, and the first of those adopted in their latter meeting at Cazenovia. (Those propositions said, 'The regeneration of the candidate constitutes his only and his sufficient title for admission into the visible church,' and 'that the title by which a person enters the visible church is the only and sufficient title for remaining in it.') For though each of the propositions may be abstractly true, and that all of them taken together might qualify the candidate for Christian fellowship, and so entitle him to admission into the church; yet a difficult point of radical importance still remains to be determined; viz., Does the applicant possess these qualifications?

What shall be deemed satisfactory evidence that he believes on the Lord Jesus Christ; that he is a subject of that regeneration, or new birth, spoken by Jesus Christ to Nicodemus? Now, if the ascertainment of these queries may be matter of very serious difficulty to the candidate himself (as it most surely may be, if we advert to daily experience and to the numerous efforts of preachers and writers to solve the anxious inquiries of doubting Christians relative to these all-important matters), how much more so must it be to those who are to be his examinators for admission. Whereas, if instead of these perplexing and almost indissoluble difficulties, teachers and churches would proceed upon the divinely prescribed practice of the Apostles; namely, to preach the gospel as heaven might grant opportunity, to every creature that had not yet professedly embraced it; and upon his being confessedly convinced and disposed to obey it, to baptize him into the name of the Father and of the Son and of the Holy Spirit, for the enjoyment of the promised salvation, as Peter did on the day of Pentecost, and afterward carefully teach the baptized to observe all things taught by the Apostles as expressly recorded in the New Testament, they would in so doing do everything as far as teaching is concerned, that God has intended to be done for the salvation of the world. And it is only by thus assuming and acting upon original ground, as we have proposed, that ever the modern churches can be reduced to New Testament order, so as to exhibit the divine costume of the apostolic churches.

"Now, if this can not be done, Christendom must remain in its apostasy; the deleterious causes and ruinous effects of which are well and truly described in the Minutes of the convention. But we can see no reason why this cannot and should not be done by a direct appeal to the divine pattern itself. . . . We make this appeal to the understanding and practice of the primitive churches, not to authorize our faith and practice, but merely to show that we understand the apostolic writings upon those subjects as they were understood from the beginning. And this we think all Christian unionists are bound to do, because it is only upon the belief of the apostolic doctrine that Christ has proposed and prayed for the unity of His people (John 17:20, 21)." Since 1839, several, if not many, other plans or methods for uniting Christians have appeared in the world. They have been made to center about doctrines that relate themselves to human creeds, experiences and character appreciation which are based upon human judgments. So they differ but little fundamentally from the method which Thomas Campbell examined and dismissed in the convincing fashion just recorded. His answer avails still for those who undervalue the plain things which constituted the apostolic message and method as the New Testament witnesses.

Chapter XVII

EDUCATION, HIGHER AND FAMILY—SLAVERY

A HOLY joy must have filled the heart of Thomas Campbell as plans for the establishment of Bethany College were talked over by the leaders, among whom he was not the least, though somewhat aged. He had been an educator; had established several academies; had helped to educate young ministers and sensed the need of both an educated ministry and constituency. On May 11, 1840, the first meeting of the Board of Trustees was called. The elder Campbell was a trustee and was unanimously called to the chair to preside over the deliberations. Again on September 18 Thomas Campbell presided at a meeting of the trustees. Both sets of minutes were signed by him as president pro tem. Probably advancing age hindered him from taking the field side by side with his son to raise funds for the embryonic institution.

The religious education of the young concerned the great church leader. He had exercised himself to bring up his own large family in the nurture and admonition of the Lord, and had been close to a large group of grandchildren and their training. It is no mere theorist therefore, who chooses the theme, "Family Education," with a subtitle, "The Nursery," and relieves himself of a burden in 1840 (*Millennial Harbinger,* p. 340). Are these not striking sentences? "Most infants from twelve to eighteen months old are capable of being instructed; so that at the age of two years they would be able to connect the idea of the heavenly Father with every object of delight and enjoyment; and thus not only become duly acquainted with the divine existence, but also with the delightful attributes of his nature—his power, wisdom, goodness and love." He stresses the need of incessant attention on the part of parents, and laments that children are seldom seen to be treated as human beings and educated by their responsible elders. He declares they are treated rather as puppets, mere playthings. "Yes, indeed, many parents (I had almost said most) take more care in training inferior animals . . . than they do in the moral and religious nature of their children; at least, for the first three, four or five years. . . . There is an indispensable necessity of family reformation *towards* God, in order to family education *for* God. . . . May the good Lord hasten family reformation." The deep concern of the writer is seen in the way he closes his production: "To the mourners in Zion"—italicized and preceded by the sign of a hand with pointing index finger. Less than a year later from the father in Israel comes "A catechetical and analytical index to the study and teaching of the Bible." At its close he uses the principles of interpretation that have become so familiar to many (not to claim that he originated them): "1st. Who speaks? 2nd. To whom does he speak?

3rd. What does he speak? Is it histories—prophecies—doctrinal declarations—commands — promises—threatenings—divine intimations, or devotional exercises? 4th. Why, when and where were these things spoken?" "A Scriptural View of the Agency of the Holy Spirit in the Conversion and Salvation of Sinners, According to the Gospel," was written by the father in 1841, and anticipated by almost two years the treatment of the subject by the son Alexander in his debate with Nathan L. Rice in Lexington, Ky. Thomas Campbell was not forced by any debate proposition to make any extreme statements, such as some profess to find in the just-mentioned debate.

In some matters the lives and attitudes and convictions of the two Campbells were so interwoven and intermingled that we can not do otherwise than treat them together. This is particularly true of the then vexatious subject of slavery. How the father had been moved to leave Kentucky, on account of conditions that attended slavery there, has been chronicled in a previous chapter. A national leader among Disciples of Christ in a public address delivered in 1934 assured his hearers that the fathers of the reformation (among whom the Campbells are ranked as chief) took no dogmatic position as to slavery, and that Alexander Campbell never owned a black man. This represents the general opinion, and is demonstrably incorrect. From *Memoirs of Alexander Campbell* (Richardson, Vol. I., pp. 501, 502), we copy these words: "As to Mr. (Alexander) Campbell's own sentiments on the subject of slavery, knowing that the relation of master and servant was recognized in the New Testament and the respective duties of the parties distinctly described, he thought it by no means inconsistent with Christian character to assume the legal rights of a master, or to transfer those rights to another, as he accordingly did in one or two instances. As he did not, however, any more than his father, approve of the abuses of power connected with the institution, those under his charge had the opportunity of learning to read and of receiving religious instruction; and furthermore, perceiving the institution as it existed in the United States to be peculiarly liable to abuses, he was always in favor of emancipation, and gave practical effect to his principles in setting free the two or three slaves he had under his control as soon as they were sufficiently grown to provide for themselves. As both father and son concurred in these views, and were determined to keep themselves free from all personal responsibility in regard to slavery, they felt themselves perfectly free to pursue their reformatory labors in any part of the country." The few slaves referred to above evidently came to Alexander Campbell with the gift of the farm by his father-in-law, when he forestalled the former's going into Ohio in a colonizing plan. The slaves' quarters are to be seen in the Campbell homestead, near Bethany. In 1829 and 1830, as a delegate to the Constitutional Convention of Virginia, Alexander Campbell opposed the position of the eastern part of Virginia which placed emphasis upon the advantage with slaveholders and slaveholding. In the latter year a slave insurrection broke out in Southampton County, Va., and in its suppression more than sixty persons were slaughtered, of whom nearly half were women and children. This happening moved the younger Campbell to write an editorial lamenting the occurrence, and to outline a plan for the gradual termination of slavery. From Jan. 1, 1834, he proposed that the sum of ten millions of dollars be set aside annually for the purchase and colonization of all people of color, slave or free, in Africa. No legislator was moved to foster the plan. In an extended tour of seventy-five days in Ohio he met with a Dr. Field, of emancipation fame, and wrote the following in his diary: "He is body, soul and spirit opposed to American slavery, and would, if he could, have one American jubilee, which would leave no room for a second. I am not sure, however, but he loves liberty even to intolerance, and would compel the churches into measures unprecedented in the days of the Apostles."

Both the Campbells found their dogmatism in opposition to the extremes of Antislavery and Abolition parties and advocates. In 1841, Cyrus McNeely, of Ohio, wrote to Thomas Campbell a copy of a letter that he was proposing to send to the brethren and churches in the slaveholding areas. It was fortunate that he sent it first to Thomas Campbell, otherwise the history of the Restoration movement might have been vastly different. The recipient took the pains to make a complete study of the Bible record as to slavery and sent same to Mr. McNeely, with the result that he saw he had been embarking on a course of unwarranted extremeness. He very wisely deferred to the judgment of his older brother in the faith. By 1845 there was much clamor for Alexander Campbell to declare himself at length upon the question of slavery. Feeling that the time was ripe, he set himself to the task of writing quite exhaustively. By way of introduction to his own series, the son requested his father to revise his reply to Mr. McNeely and made use of the same. The following paragraphs indicate the position taken: "Upon the whole, with reference to American slavery, wherever distinguished by any inhuman and anti-Christian adjuncts, we may justly and reasonably conclude that as Christianity and truly moralized humanity prevail, it must and will go down; and that in these respects, no Christian can either approve or practice it. It may also provoke God to destroy it more speedily by terrible judgments, as in the case of Egypt, Babylon, Nineveh and Jerusalem, wholly destroyed on account of their cruelty and oppression. Wherefore it becomes the American people, both as citizens and Christians, to consider these things and to so discharge their duties for the amelioration and ultimate abolition of slavery; especially those of them that have embraced the gospel." Appended to the letter goes the following note from Alexander, the admiring son: "The preceding document we have thought might not be unacceptable to many of our readers in this period of excitement and extremes upon a very exciting subject. It is the calm, considerate and candid reasonings and conclusions of one of the most disinterested of mankind —an octogenarian of sound mind and discriminating judgment—well-read in sacred literature—and, in my opinion, as pure a philanthropist as breathes. He has long thought upon the subject. The crisis calling upon me for some remarks upon this theme, I have thought good to preface my remarks by a re-publication of this document." The editor of the *Harbinger* used as his subject "Our Position to American Slavery." He made comments on a written debate that was being carried on between Dr. Wayland, of Brown University, and Dr. Richard Fuller, of South Carolina, as he set forth his position. But the aged Campbell was not silent, for he wrote a reply to "A Disciple on Slavery," and found time to write on "Laws and Duties of Matrimony" also. In an editorial (*Millennial Harbinger*, p. 233, 1845) Alexander Campbell mentions the actual threatening divisions among the Methodists and Presbyterians over slavery, and thus declares himself: "For myself, I greatly prefer the condition and the prospects of the free to the slave states; especially as respects the whole portion of their population. . . . Our position is not that of a politician, an economist, a mere moralist, but that of a Christian." Numerous other quotations could be cited to indicate and prove that the Campbells did not sidestep their responsibility in

EDUCATION, HIGHER AND FAMILY—SLAVERY 189

helping to show the people the way out of slavery. Was it the overruling providence of God, the soundness of mind of the Campbells and other leaders, the willingness of disciples of both North and South to be led, that enabled them to come through the forties, fifties and sixties and not divide into "North Disciples" and "South Disciples"? What a great sentence is this: "Christians can never be reformers in any system which uses violence, recommends or expects it"! It comes from 1845.

Chapter XVIII

ZEALOUS EVEN UNTO DEATH

DURING a visit to Bethany, J. R. Frame, an evangelist, of Ohio, proposed to Thomas Campbell a period of joint service among the churches in Ohio. He took the same under advisement and replied under date May 16, 1843. Consider a few sentences: "I should be very glad to co-operate with you in this good work, for all the purposes you mentioned when you were here; but my son, Alexander, is quite opposed to my proceeding any farther in itinerant labors at my advanced age of eighty years. He rather urges the application of my time to writing, and to local labors in the vicinity of Bethany. However, what I shall do I have not yet finally determined. But if I conclude to co-operate with you a part of this summer, I shall endeavor to be with you at the time and place above mentioned." His love for preaching and the fellowship of brethren and churches that he had been instrumental in establishing in the gospel way led him to disregard his son's objections, and he met Mr. Frame at the appointed time and place. The two directed their way through Guernsey, Muskingum and Washington Counties of Ohio. Father Campbell at times preached sermons of two hours' duration. Baptists, Disciples, Cumberlands and others received them gladly. Many were strengthened in the faith, and not a few converts were made. During this period the aged pilgrim received what is termed "second sight," and was able to discard his spectacles. At one place he was delayed by a sudden illness, but after a few days he was able to resume his schedule of travel and preaching. "The good and pious example of Father Campbell did much to promote the cause of reformation on this tour of two months. Also much prejudice was removed from the mind of many who had misunderstood and misrepresented the reformation" (*Memoirs of Elder Thomas Campbell,* pp. 290-3).

From a private letter of Mr. Campbell that was written on Jan. 17, 1844, and which was so well thought of that it was given place in the *Harbinger* of May, 1845, we quote: "Dear Brother: I am much gratified with the account of your labors and of their success, especially among our Baptist brethren, between whom and us there never should have been any difference; nor indeed, would there, had it not been for a few proud partizans in the Redstone Association, of which once we were all members. The reformation which we propose as defined in the fourth page of our Declaration and Address, published at Washington, Pa., November, 1809, expressly excludes the teaching of anything as matter of the Christian faith or duty for which there can not be expressly produced a 'thus saith the Lord,' either in express terms or by approved precedent. Upon these propositions the Baptists at first cordially received us; and some years afterwards were excited to reject us, not for any alleged departure from the said propositions, but because we would not adopt the Philadelphia Confession of Faith as our standard, which we could not consistently do, being expressly contrary to our avowed principles, which we had conscientiously adopted, as the only scriptural ground of union; nevertheless, we have always considered and treated them as brethren as far as they would permit us; and as far as I am concerned, always intend to do so. And in the meantime we would humbly advise you so to treat them. And, of course, to do anything in your power to build up and pacify their societies. The church of Christ upon earth is constitutionally and essentially one; therefore the first relative duty of every member of it is to preserve this unity, by loving each other as Christ has loved them; for this is the divinely appointed badge of genuine discipleship (John 13: 34). Dear Brother: Christian union upon Christian principles is our motto, our object. Now to perfect this union in faith and holiness ought to be our grand concern. For what is profession without possession?" This letter is valuable as a testimony that Thomas Campbell was as sure then as at the beginning that he had discovered the way out of division.

"An address to all our Christian brethren upon the necessity and importance of the actual enjoyment of our holy religion" indicates that Thomas Campbell was no stranger to "heartfelt religion," nor was he adverse to its possession by all. The production entitled as above was written in 1844. See him defining the word "all" in the title— "all, however diversified by professional epithets, those accidental distinctions which have unhappily and unscripturally diversified the believing world." And whom does he reckon as "our Christian brethren"? Quotation: "By our Christian brethren, then, we mean the very same description of character addressed in our Declaration, published at Washington, Pa., in the year 1809; namely, all that love our Lord Jesus Christ in sincerity throughout the churches! If there were none at that time throughout the churches, then Christianity was dead and gone. And if there be none such at present within the same limits, it still continues extinct." In all his long life of advocating Christian union, Thomas Campbell had no feeling that he was inconsistent in granting to individuals and churches the use of the name "Christian," while at the same time he sought to make them more Christian by having them fill up that which was lacking in their fulfillment of scriptural requirements and dismiss from both individual and church life all that exceeded "what was written." Love of the brethren did not blind the advocate of Christian union to loyalty to the Lord and sponsor of brotherliness.

In the now oft-quoted *Millennial Harbinger* (1845, p. 231) stands a letter from Thomas Campbell to N. H. Finney, that deserves to be well known. Mr. Finney was a converted infidel, and he and some others had conceived the idea of going into New England to evangelize, and Father Campbell essayed some advice as to their procedure. This quotation is possibly the last treatment by Thomas Campbell of the subject of baptism: "What a pity that Christians should be divided by a difference about baptism, which is the very door of the church, by which we enter into the one family, under the one Father! A difference which lies at the very commencement, yea, at the very foundation of our Christian profession! For no person was considered a Christian in the apostolic churches who had not confessed Christ as his Lord and Saviour in baptism. See Rom. 6: 3-7, with Gal. 3: 26, 27, etc. And this difference not only about the action to be performed, but also about the proper subject of it! Alas! alas! this radical evil. But we can not help it. All that we can do is to show from the good Book that neither the action nor the subject is left indefinite, but the former* is always a believer; and the latter* such a use of water as represents a burial; namely, an immersion. But this radical evil is not the only thing that affects Christian unity. There are many other unscriptural notions and opinions, which have unhappily destroyed Christian unity, which must be obviated; either by showing that they are not divinely inculcated either as a matter of Christian faith or duty; or by showing that if what is expressly inculcated for these purposes were truly realized, these notions and opinions could be of no service; for that everything which they are supposed to effect would be perfect without them; so that they could *be of no use, there would be no room for them.* The former method I should prefer for public popular teaching; though the latter* might be useful in private conversation; or in cases of argumentation; but the less of this the better, if we can consistently avoid it."

Thomas M. Henley, who had labored and suffered much for the cause of reformation in Virginia, died in 1846. Shortly before his death he had sent the following message to Alexander Campbell: "After a correspondence of nearly twenty-one years, I am the more persuaded of the great work you are engaged in, and that no man or set of men can ever publish a more solid basis of union than you and your venerable father have published to the world some thirty-five years ago." Not all at that time were remembering the part that the father had in projecting the new-old cause of Christian union. And so with some even today.

It is recorded that in the spring of 1846, Thomas Campbell felt moved to set forth on an itinerary of the churches. All went well for a time, but he had overestimated his strength, and in the summer he made his way home greatly exhausted and affected by the heat. Then his friends insisted that he suspend all further excursions distant

---

*There is in this sentence a peculiar use of "former" and "latter"—just the reverse from present-day common use. Alexander Campbell makes a similar use of the two words in "Christian System" (fourth edition: 1867). The double use in this same letter which we are quoting shows that it was not the lapse of an aged mind.

from home. He yielded to their importunities and settled down among his relatives, manuscripts and books. From a letter to a daughter, dated July 6, 1847, we cull the following: "My sight is so dim that I must quit writing. . . . In looking over my old religious manuscripts, I have selected a few of them for publication in *The Millennial Harbinger*. . . . I shall take the liberty of directing your attention to a few hymns in our common hymn book, which, I humbly think, claim our practical attention as so many gospel feasts." Such was the beautiful, gentle nature of their grandfather that the children of Alexander Campbell vied with each other in rendering service to him and making his last days as happy as possible.

There was a general feeling that the old man's life might be crowned with a farewell appearance in the church house at Bethany and an opportunity to speak. So it was arranged that on Jan. 1, 1851, Thomas Campbell should go to church and speak. A very large audience was present, among whom were found thirty young ladies from the near-by Pleasant Hill Seminary, conducted by the McKeevers, at Independence, Pa. Afraid of that which was high, Mr. Campbell was conducted to the church on a horse-drawn sled. He was enfeebled in body and impaired somewhat in memory, but he delivered a very creditable message, which was reproduced by Professor Pendleton, and is to be found in *"Memoirs of Thomas Campbell."* Total blindness set in about this same time, but even that did not mar the sweetness of the man who was soon to be ninety years of age. Friends delighted to come and converse with him. His mind was able to the end to reproduce favorite passages of Scripture and stanzas of hymns. He cheered himself and others with that Word which he had found light and food and drink to his soul in the memorable decades of his life.

It was on Jan. 4, 1854, in the Campbell home, that Thomas Campbell yielded up his soul unto its faithful Creator and Saviour. Out of the imperfect, struggling, divided church he moved into the perfected, resting and united church of the firstborn on high. "Gone, but not forgotten" can well belong to him as an epitaph. For who could forget the man who raised the slogan, "Let us unite as Christians" when it was the height of heresy to think of any such thing, and kept crying aloud until others caught the echo and whose slogan has become church-wide and world-wide? His earthly remains were placed in the Campbell Cemetery near to Bethany, beside those of his wife. Goodly numbers go annually to that sacred spot guarded by waving evergreens to look upon Thomas Campbell's earthly resting place. But they will have to travel the world around and make incursions to all types of Christian faith to see measurably the living influence of the American advocate of Christian union.

Chapter XIX

SOME TRIBUTES FROM ADMIRERS

AS the word of the death of Thomas Campbell passed throughout the fellowship a wave of sorrow passed over all. Yet the sorrow was turned into joy as all considered that his lifework was done, and that he had entered into the rest and reward of God's faithful. From all sections of the world there came to Bethany messages that spoke appreciatively of the character and labors of the departed. But it was not in the mind of Alexander, the son, to magnify the deserving father, therefore he gave but a few of the messages to the general public. In the *Memoirs* of his father, he wrote no chapter concerning the last illness and death. He used rather the obituary notice which Dr. Richardson prepared for the *Harbinger,* and included the detailed notice of his father's last illness and death, written by Mrs. Selina H. Campbell (the son's wife) and sent to Editor Challen for insertion in the *Christian Annual.*

From an intimate association of several decades with the father Campbell, Dr. Richardson, who had been his pupil in Pittsburgh in boyhood days as well as a colleague in preaching and editing in later days, writes: "Never was there an individual who manifested greater reverence for the Word of God, or a truer desire to see it obeyed faithfully. Yet this trust in the divine Word was not, with him, a mere verbal confidence, a faith or knowledge, like that of some professors, merely intellectual—lexical and grammatical; for never was there one who more fully recognized the spirituality of the gospel, or sought more diligently to impress all around him with the importance of the work of the Holy Spirit in the salvation of the soul; and never was there one who more fully exemplified the doctrine which he taught, or whose life was more evidently guided by the teachings of the Spirit, and controlled by the divine principle of love to God and man. To the faith of Abraham and the piety of Samuel, he added the knowledge, the purity and warm affections of the Christian, and combined in his deportment a simplicity of manners and a courtesy singularly graceful, with a dignity which inspired with respect all who approached him." In his *Memoirs of Alexander Campbell,* Richardson gives but two pages to the death of Thomas Campbell, and makes use of a letter of the son Alexander to a Brother Dungan in Baltimore. In that same occurs this estimate: "I never knew a man in all my acquaintance with men, of whom it could have been said with more assurance that '*he walked with God.*' Such was the even tenor of his path, not for a few years, but a period as far back as my memory reaches; and that is on the other side of a half century. How many say: 'Let me die the death of the righteous, and let my last days be like his,' who, nevertheless, do not choose to live his life!"r

There appeared in the *Ladies' Christian Annual,* published in Philadelphia in 1854, an account of a visit paid to the aged Thomas Campbell, by James Challen, possibly late in 1853. He relates that he heard him lead family prayers, listened to his recitation of Bible verses and hymns ("How happy are they who their Saviour obey," being one of his great favorites), marked his keen interest and belief in matters connected with the life eternal. "He has one of the finest heads I ever saw. Phrenology would claim it as a model, both for its conformation and size; and the volume of the brain is very great. Though so very old, his skin has all the freshness and beauty of youth. His cheeks have but few wrinkles and are quite full. Nis noble brow is almost entirely smooth. . . . He is the patriarch of the reformation, the Jacob of the tribes, a type and representative of what we mean by a disciple of Christ, an exemplification of the truth and beauty of apostolic Christianity, of its spirituality and life, of the faith it inspires, the hope which it awakens, and the immortal principles which it inculcates. I would advise the self-constituted judges of orthodoxy to pay him a visit and learn to abate their zeal for an antiquated and toothless theology. I would urge the devotees of an empty, dry and bony ritualism to visit Bethany House and take a few lessons from this aged disciple and family on the value of that religion which is both spirit and truth. And to the philosophic mystics of the day, the super-spiritualized, whose highest evidence of their interest in Christ consists in their contempt for those who differ from them, and the conscious self-complacency which they feel, I would commend a visit, in the confident belief that, if their cases are not utterly hopeless, the result will prove beneficial.''

When Alexander Campbell set himself, in 1860, to write the memoirs of his father, he secured several appreciative letters from former fellow workers. Among them was one from the beloved Walter Scott. It was quite characteristic, and deserves to be better known than it is. Mr. Scott was living then in Mayslick, Ky. He wrote to Mrs. Bryant, daughter of the lamented father, dating his letter May 8, 1860. "Mrs. Bryant: Very Dear Sister—The Lord bless you and yours! The Lord make you a blessing to many people! . . . Touching the matter whereof you write to me, I am, I regret to say, in possession of no documents or incidents that you would deem of any value in a biography of Father Campbell. Both of our families resided for some time in different apartments of the same house, he and I taught the same school, and presided together as bishops in the same church (Pittsburgh), and, therefore, upon continuous reflection, some incidents might occur to my mind which time has long obliterated. I made the acquaintance of your brother Alexander in 1821-2, and soon after that had the pleasure, at his suggestion, I presume, of a visit from your dear and venerable father. In his case, as in that of his son, we at once conceived an ardent Christian affection for each other, which, by the way, continued uninterrupted and unabated while he tarried on earth. Alas! where now is the venerable man, the man of God, and the holy ones who, under his pastoral care, among the cabins of western Pennsylvania and western Virginia, worshiped the God of our salvation? Gone, all gone,

> And left us weeping on the shore
> To which they will return no more.

. . . Since Father Campbell was so much better known to you all than to me, it would be improper in me to attempt, for your benefit, a description of his excellencies, either intellectual, moral, social or religious; and yet I may, perhaps, state in a few words, without presumption, how he appeared to me under these several phases.

"I always regarded your father as a man of fine intellectual parts. The evidence of this was derived to me from two sources—sense and reason, the eye and the ear. It was impossible to look upon his lofty brow and facial lines of thought without reading in these exterior symbols intellectual greatness—reason, robust common sense, capacity, skill, wisdom. 'The trial of a man is his speech,' says the son of Sirach. Your father's public efforts fully vindicated, by the apocalypse he made of truth, all first impressions. Sometimes he spoke with great effect; and though he often protracted his speech to a great length—the manners and the taste of the times demanding it—yet he did not do so always. I heard him in my academy, which was large, deliver a current commentary of James, first chapter; and can say, in regard to it, that I have not, since that time, listened to anything in the way of teaching more beautiful in expression, or in thought and reason more delightful and ravishing.

"He was fond of discussion, and frequently offered propositions for debate. On such occasions he was a little sensitive and high-spirited. Amid the affray of words and arguments which his genius for dialectics had waked up, he ever held his old gold snuff-box in his hand, and snatching thence, at unequal intervals, "a hasty pinch" of the good old Scotch, as Henry Clay called it, he would immediately renew the conflict with increased energy.

"He was, of course, fond of headwork. His intellectual system could not lay idle. He engaged its forces in various ways, therefore by abstract thought, reflection, meditation, lucubration, contemplation and excogitation; so that sometimes he looked pensive, sad, cast down, melancholy. Such appeared to me, intellectually, your pious and enlightened father. Those who think your brother's strong intellectual qualities were not derived to him from his father, differ from me *toto caelo*.

"Touching his practical nature, its basis seemed *moral* rather than *sentient*. His affections were, therefore, stirred from within rather than from without, and shone forth in respect for the rights of others, rather than in excitability for their faults. He was patient more than impressible;

meek, gentle and resigned, more than passionate or easily provoked. He wished well to all the world, whose salvation he desired and loved with unspeakable complacency his neighbors, his family and the saints.

"Though his nature, as I have said, was affectionate rather than sensitive, yet his sympathies could be stirred up to floods of tears by the occasion; and of this, the following is proof: Our preaching had, one day, taken such fast hold on the heart of a certain lady as to produce a slight alienation of mind, which, on our return, we learned had continued for a week. At the end of that time, on a second visit, many people offered themselves for the obedience of faith, and were baptized. In the conclusion of the beautiful scene, said lady pushed herself close up to my side, until indeed she almost leaned upon me. All the people saw her, and every heart was touched, for she spoke not a word. Father Campbell stood as close to my person almost as the lady herself. Looking upon the countenance of my venerable co-laborer, I said to him: 'My dear father, if the word of God has perturbed the soul of this poor lady, may not the same word also, under other circumstances, tranquilize it?' 'Brother Scott,' he replied, 'baptize her.' Turning to the woman, I took the confession and asked her if she repented of her sins. Without lifting her eyes from the ground, on which they were fixed, she replied, 'I have repented most wonderfully.' On the utterance of these extraordinary words, a flood of tears gushed from the eyes of my venerable associate, as if his head had been a fountain of water. They absolutely fell in a stream to the ground. The memory of the fact must remain with me through life. I baptized the lady, and, thanks be to God, she awoke next morning in full possession of her senses. . . .

"Touching his religion, he was the most devout man I ever knew. He loved God, and adored him for the gift of his Son in our great redemption. He was a man of prayer, a man of reading, a man of holy meditation, excogitation and reformation. He was fond of the analogies between the two divine systems, nature and religion, and read with delight in the works of God, the spiritual relations of the universe. He ascended from infinite power to infinite wisdom, from infinite wisdom to infinite goodness, and read and realized in the things that are seen, the things that are not seen, but yet are eternal. All things he saw with delight were made for man and man for his Maker. He ascended then, by nature and religion, up to the God of nature and religion. He had tasted of the sovereign and universal good, and his heart was in the heavens. He was the most exemplary man I ever saw. His memory is blessed. WALTER SCOTT."

Either the daughter who received the above letter or the son who used it in the "*Memoirs*" of his father, was unwilling to let pass Mr. Scott's reference to the "old gold snuff-box." On the page where the same occurs it is followed by an asterisk, and it guides to the sentence at the bottom of the page, "*He gave up the use of snuff for nearly thirty years before his death." If Thomas Campbell had followed the liberty and custom of the times for the clergy, he might have been a user of intoxicating liquors, as well as of snuff. But all evidence points to his having been a total abstainer.

Evidently his co-laborer felt that Mr. Campbell might have been much briefer in his remarks on many occasions. He is very kind in writing "he often protracted his speech to a great length." Archibald McLean writes: "With all his estimable qualities, it would seem that Thomas Campbell must have been somewhat tedious at times. This appears when we recall that he took an hour to read a hymn and two or three hours for the sermon that followed." This was not a fault of old age, for on one occasion when he was yet a student in divinity, and being home for a season, Thomas led the family devotions. His father at the time was afflicted with rheumatism in his knees, and the son failed to remember this fact. He lost himself in a prayer so long that it turned his father's devotion into anger. When at a long last, the budding minister uttered the "Amen" and all rose to their feet, he was no doubt completely surprised to feel his father's cane on his back. The sound caning did not make of Thomas Campbell a pray-er of short prayers, nor a preacher of short sermons, nor a director of short services. But we recall that he belonged to an age that seemed to expect and could stand messages measured by hours rather than by minutes.

Chapter XX

CHARACTER—CONSISTENCY—THE FELLOWSHIP

UNDER a section in *Memoirs of Elder Thomas Campbell,* the son wrote ten pages of an appreciative nature, pointing out the striking and worthy characteristics and activities of his father. These open with "a supreme devotion to truth" and include such things as an unselfish and self-sacrificing spirit; unfeigned piety and free and familiar communion with God; habits of Bible study; deadness to the world and its political agitations; averseness to evil-speaking and reproach; exaltation of religion and morality; unremitting efforts to unite Christians on a scriptural and evangelical basis; hospitality to strangers and assiduity in searching out good to be done; thoroughgoing consistency; high consciousness in the work of the ministry. It is believed that what has been included in the foregoing pages fully establishes the clear title of Mr. Campbell to all that his son assigns to him. Alexander Campbell was not indulging in an admiring son's panegyrics.

Attention should be called to the fact that Thomas Campbell never stood in the way of the young. He ever kept a youthful heart and wisely felt that place must be given to an oncoming generation of ministers. So from the time that he undertook the theological training of his oldest son and two others in the Christian Association days, he encouraged the young to prepare themselves and speak out. He was able to save several young ministers for a lifetime ministry by championing their cause against the older ministers who would have squelched and silenced them. There was always a freshness and appositeness to both the spoken and written messages of Mr. Campbell. He bore on his heart the constant improvement of churches and the ministry.

This present critical age must bear witness to the clarity of vision, both mental and spiritual, of our subject. Whether defending himself in the heresy trial, or advocating Christian union and apostolic Christianity, he was neither foggy nor muddy in ideas. In an age which believed in and entrenched itself behind a level Bible, Mr. Campbell discerned and advocated the Testaments of the Bible, maintaining the superiority of the New over the Old. There was an Old Testament church and an Old Testament authority over it; and a New Testament church with its corresponding authority, the New Testament. In this latter church the Lord Jesus Christ stood alone as supreme as the apostolic testimony unvaryingly maintained. From this position of supremacy the Christ ought not be dislodged and the unity of the church was natural and essential. The creeds which men fashioned supplanted Christ and helped to create and maintain division among Christians. He saw as a way to reunion and unbroken fellowship among believers a re-assessment of the place of Christ and the apostles in the church and a devaluation of creeds "of human composure" as tests and bonds of fellowship. He set Christ in and over the entire church without apology in true Pauline fashion, and registered his dependence absolutely upon the apostolic writings for knowledge of the life and revelation and will of Jesus Christ.

It has appeared that there were times of depression and discouragement in the life of Thomas Campbell. Men were so reluctant to receive what to him had such rightful claim both scripturally and logically upon all Christians. With great alacrity it seemed to him all Christians ought to have heeded after they had heard. It grieved him that partisans and parties, ministers and ministered to, would steel their hearts against what was so plainly written in what they acknowledged to be the Word of God. However, through it all he continued in great patience. He consistently refused to vitiate his essential New Testament plan for union by a compromise that would carry into the newly established churches things that rested on human traditions, no matter how ancient they were nor how almost universally received. Centuries of straying from the New Testament model of the church could not be remedied in a few decades. But a beginning could be made of a return to the apostolic ideals, and time would accelerate the movement.

Efforts have been made by some who look upon themselves as champions of the movement inaugurated by Thomas Campbell to claim that he was favorable to a Christian union which left such subjects as baptism in the realm of private judgment; in more modern terminology, Christian union by "open membership" and "the equality of all Christians before God," each sect and individual assessing itself and himself. And so he was in the period of the Christian Association of Washington. Facts warrant the even further statement that he was favorable to a Christian union which had sprinkling for baptism and infant baptism as a church ordinance, for such was the actual condition of the Christian Association. But it must be remembered that Thomas Campbell had uttered the slogan, "Where the Scriptures speak, we speak; where the Scriptures are silent, we are silent." This committed him and his associates to the Scriptures and to them alone. Later he (or they) issued the "Declaration and Address" which most definitely set up principles which were to eliminate everything that was not biblical, and as old as the apostles' testimony, from church life. The Christian Associationists did not stultify themselves by refusing to walk in the way that they had chosen, and that way brought advance and change. The Christian Association became a church of Christ. The erstwhile infant-sprinkled Christians "got themselves baptized" (Goodspeed's New Testament phrase), for they were led by the Bible to see that nothing but immersion was baptism in New Testament times. The action of pious parents, the act authorized by pope and creeds, could have no standing before the fact that the Christ, the

Scriptures had spoken. It is unfair to Thomas Campbell to present as representative his attitude before he had come to see the reach and necessary result of his motto and principles. These were the light by which he advanced into becoming an immersed believer in Christ, bearing only the name of Christian and disciple of the Christ, eschewing all sectarianism in the church and advocating the union of the church and the conversion of the world. The writer has been unable to discover in any of the ministry or writings of Thomas Campbell, after he had settled the baptismal question for himself, any act or word that can be used as warrant for the omission of the immersion of believers from his plan for Christian union. That plan was *in the truth* and *on the Bible.*

In his early ministry for union the people of the Baptist persuasion were looked upon as the most-ripe prospects for his message. Doubtless this, because they were right on the act which is baptism, were congregational in polity and less bound by creed. It was a Pauline procedure, Baptists taking the place of "Jews" in the phrase "to the Jews first." The Baptists were nearer to the New Testament ideal, as Jews were nearer than Gentiles to being Christians. It has been seen in some of the latest writings of Mr. Campbell, as they have been incorporated in this work, that he pays this tribute to the Baptists. He had a concern for their churches which does not appear for other Christian bodies as such. These latter had much greater and many more steps to take that they might measure up as reformed and restored churches of Christ.

There exists in the world today a body of people (if such loosely related units can be termed a body) that bears the name "Disciples of Christ," "Christian Churches" or "Churches of Christ," and numbers almost one million and a half members in all the world; also another body (very loosely related likewise) of almost half a million, which calls itself "Churches of Christ." Both these sets of people hark back to the motto and Declaration and Address of Thomas Campbell. Three main points of cleavage between the two peoples are the name, the system of settled pastors and instrumental music in the public worship of the churches. The irony of the situation appears in that while Thomas Campbell desired to form no party, yet a party came into existence. Was this not rather natural and necessary? There was no sect or party in existence that desired to be plainly and entirely biblical. The call for people to become and be so, really established the party, unless those who were persuaded remained in their unscriptural party. This seems to parallel the situation in the church at Corinth of which the apostle Paul writes in 1 Corinthians, chapters 1 and 3. Those who did not claim to be "of Paul" or "of Apollos" or "of Cephas" were left to be, or claim to be, or to vaunt themselves as "of Christ." These last were right in not wanting to be anything else than "of Christ," for Paul closed the first chapter with the words, "But of him are ye in Christ Jesus, who was made unto us wisdom from God, and righteousness and sanctification and redemption: that according as it is written, He that glorieth, let him glory in the Lord." And in this fashion the apostle closes the third chapter: "Wherefore let no one glory in men. For all things are yours; whether Paul, or Apollos, or Cephas, or the world, or life, or death, or things present, or things to come; all are yours and ye are Christ's; and Christ is God's." There might have been something unworthy in the way in which those Corinthian Christians were trying to be "of Christ," and so they were entitled to rebuke, but the fact that they were "of Christ" was natural, and represented that to which the three parties had to return. They had to abandon glorying in men and return to glorying in the Lord. That was the only way in which partyism in Corinth could be eliminated. Such was the vision of the nineteenth-century advocate of Christian union, and he had caught it from that first-century champion on unity in Christ.

This present-day party to end parties among Christians finds within its ranks large numbers who have followed Thomas Campbell as he felt he was following Christ, by renouncing creeds and denominational names, by procuring a baptism that is biblical and not traditional, by holding to the New Testament as the Book of rule and discipline, by urging upon other Christians union upon the Bible. Occurrences have not been uncommon of entire congregations adjusting their private faith and public procedure so as to become churches of

Christ, as happened in the lifetime of Thomas
Campbell, especially among Baptist churches.
Were he to return to earth, probably his first
ministry would be among the two peoples who are
so near together because they have looked to
him under Christ.

Chapter XXI

THE PLEA AND PLAN: AMEND OR ADOPT?

IN the century and a quarter since 1809, there have sprung into existence several scores of new sects and parties, denominations and communions, under the Christian banner. So what? The older Christianity becomes, the more plagued by partyism does it become? The more Christian union is advocated, the more it is disregarded and shown to be impossible of attainment? In a sense, there is a gain in the very multiplication of divisions, for it demonstrates that human creeds are unable to unite Christians. So was the contention of Thomas Campbell. The Apostles' Creed, the Athanasian Creed, the Lutheran Creed, the Schmalkald Articles, the Westminster Confession of Faith, the Thirty-nine Articles of Religion, the Methodist Discipline, the Philadelphia Confession of Faith— not to mention others, determined orthodoxy and declared heterodoxy, but division has followed in the wake of all. And in the last century there has been a gradual weakening of the use of creeds as tests of faith and bonds of fellowship. Not only are church members quite often excused from knowing and subscribing to the creed, but even ministers in creedal churches hold themselves in numerous cases above and beyond the creed. So it is that church members and ministers are left free to make quite free, if not sole use of the Scriptures as the book for faith. This was a cardinal desire and principle of Thomas Campbell. "Thine own wickedness shall correct thee, and thy backslidings shall reprove thee," declared Jeremiah in the long ago (Jer. 2:19). The unity that was the yearning ideal of Jesus the Christ and the goal of the apostolic ministers has been turned into the disunity that has weakened Christianity, that has become a rock of offense to believers and unbelievers, that has wasted our substance and shortened our vision. The wickedness of division among Christians and backsliding from the union ideals of the Head of the church are set to correct us and reprove us until we return. In a century of multiplying divisions there has been an increasing cry for remedying the evils of division and establishing union. Only here and there will be lifted a dissonant and anachronistic voice which thanks God for our divisions and glorifies Him as the author of religious confusion. The breaking up of denominations and the breaking down of denominational walls would seem to be incidental to the making of one fellowship, one church, not a huge ecclesiasticism, but in Christ.

Furthermore, the last century has witnessed the coming to the fore of many plans to disarm, ally and unite Christians. The projection of the Evangelical Alliance in London in 1846, came too late to receive the vigorous mental attention of Thomas Campbell. Its aim was to ally for action; not to unite, as against the Campbellian method of the dissolution and ending of denominations. The second doctrinal article of the Alliance insisted on the right and duty of private judgment as to the Scriptures, and the succeeding articles vitiate that right by specifying things about the Trinity, total depravity, justification by faith alone and so on. The Evangelical Alliance felt obligated to pay tribute to theological systems and the deliverances of the creeds. It was open to the same objections that Mr. Campbell had lodged against the union effort in New York in 1838 and 1839. The Federal Council of Churches of Christ in America was established in 1908 to act for twenty-eight Protestant bodies in matters of common interest, but the great matter of Christian union seems forestalled by the recognition of the bodies as fixed, unchanging entities. Indeed the organization sometimes seems to make demands that call for setting aside the word of the Scriptures. There have been conferences on faith and order, on the manufacture of new creeds, but always the salvaging of denominations has stood in the way of great advance and results.

Since the death of Thomas Campbell there have been accomplished the union of some several religious bodies in parts of the whole world. Various motives have entered to determine methods and results, and there has nearly always been left behind one or more dissatisfied groups. These can scarcely be termed unions on the Bible, for they have too often perpetuated one or more denominational names and have continued an old or formulated a new creed. There have been great religious bodies seeking for years to heal the divisions incident to the Civil War. A larger denomination would result, but would leave the question of the gathering together of all the fragmentary peoples of Jesus Christ untouched. The followers of Christ out in distant lands that are largely virgin to Christianity have had to face the problems of union and have striven in one way or another to get together and present a united front to other religions and cultures. An inherent weakness has been an over-emphasis on the creedal, and an under-emphasis on the clear voice of Jesus Christ in the Scriptures.

The eternal God alone knows how much Thomas Campbell, lifting up his pen and voice for Christian union in 1809, is responsible for present-day sentiment for and conviction as to the confluence of the followers of the Son of God. It may be much or little, but there is a live question that can not be allowed to lie unanswered. It is this: Is Thomas Campbell's plan and method for the union of Christians valid for today? He desired "an entire union of all the churches, in faith and practice, according to the word of God." It was to him "a pleasing consideration that all the churches of Christ which mutually acknowledge each other as such, are not only agreed in the great doctrines of faith and holiness, but are also materially agreed as to the positive ordinances of the gospel institution; so that our differences, at most, are about the things in which the kingdom of God does not consist;

THE PLEA AND PLAN: AMEND OR ADOPT? 219

that is, about matters of private opinion or human invention. What a pity that the kingdom of God should be divided about such things." Was Thomas Campbell proud and ambitious of personal fame? "Our dear brethren of all denominations will please to consider that we have our educational prejudices and particular customs to struggle against as well as they. But this we do sincerely declare, that there is nothing we have hitherto received as matters of faith or practice, which is not expressly taught and enjoined in the word of God, either in express terms or approved precedent, that we would not heartily relinquish, that so we might return to the original constitutional unity of the Christian church; and in this happy unity, enjoy full communion with all our brethren in peace and charity." And how his heart burned within him as he touched upon the way! "You are all, dear brethren, equally included as objects of our love and esteem. With you all we desire to unite in the bonds of an entire Christian unity—Christ alone being the *head*, the center; his word the *rule;* an explicit belief of and manifest conformity to it, in all things—*the terms*. More than this, you will not require of us; and less we can not require of you; nor, indeed, can we reasonably suppose any would desire it, for what good purpose would it serve? We dare neither assume nor propose the trite indefinite distinction between essentials and non-essentials, in matters of revealed truth and duty; firmly persuaded, that, whatever may be their comparative importance, simply considered, the high obligation of the divine authority revealing or enjoining them, renders the belief or performance of them absolutely essential to us, in so far as we know them. And to be ignorant of anything God has revealed can neither be our duty or our privilege."

And what audacity! The voice of Thomas Campbell and a few others calling to large denominations of Christians! "And we again beseech you, let it be known that it is the invitation of but a few; by your accession we shall be many; and, whether few or many, in the first instance, it is all one with respect to the event which must ultimately await the full information and concurrence of all. Besides, whatever is to be done, must begin sometime, somewhere, and no matter where, nor by whom, if the Lord puts his hand to the work, it must surely prosper. And has he not been graciously pleased, upon many signal occasions, to bring to pass the greatest events from very small beginnings, and even by means of the most unlikely? Duty then is ours; but events belong to God."*

That the idea of authority bulks too large in the plan of Thomas Campbell may be an objection to it in these days when the word "authority" is too often uttered with a sneer. Our generation might humbly meditate on the thesis that it is wrong on the subject of obedience. No one can study the records of the life of Jesus Christ and with fairness miss the idea of authority. He recognized His duty to obey God. He called Himself Lord and

*Quotations from "Declaration and Address."

fastened obedience to himself upon his disciples. A test of their love for him was obedience to his commandments. In his own mind, he, Jesus, was the sovereign, commanding, authoritative Lord and Christ. The writing apostles bear testimony that they received him as such. God had made him (Jesus Christ) "head over all things to the church." The gospel and its preaching came by him who said, "All authority in heaven and on earth has been given unto me." Grace and apostleship were given unto Paul of Tarsus unto the obedience of faith among all the nations for the sake of Jesus' name. Christ was the Head of every man and subjection to him a jeweled virtue. It would seem that if the plan of Christian union, which was the burden of the latter part of Mr. Campbell's life, is defective and unsuited to our times, it borrowed its defects from Jesus the Christ and his apostles; and its unsuitability attaches to our unwillingness to humble ourselves under the mighty hand of God. We do well to use to the full the Christian union method of him whose life we have been studying, until some one proposes a better.

Thomas Campbell, of you we say with J. N. Maffitt:

> Fallen, a holy man of God,
> An Israelite indeed,
> A standard-bearer of the cross,
> Mighty in word and deed;
> A master spirit of the age,
> A bright and burning light,
> Whose beams across the firmament
> Scattered the clouds of night!

Thomas Campbell, of your great purpose and burning desire, we say with M. C. Kurfees:

> How blest and how joyous will be the glad day,
>   When heart beats to heart in the work of the Lord;
> When Christians united shall swell the grand lay,
>   "Divisions all ended, triumphant his Word."
>
> Oh! shout the glad word, oh! hasten the day
>   When all of God's people are one.

THE END.